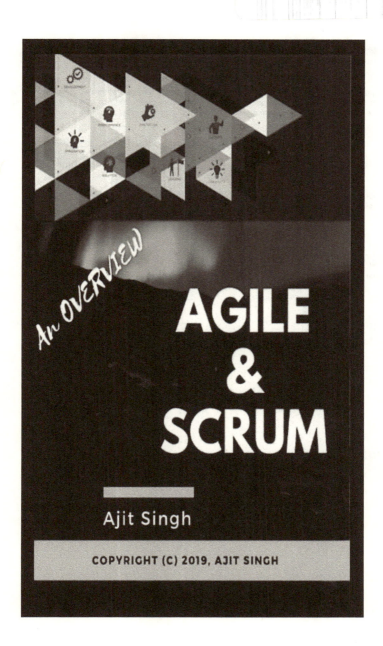

An OVERVIEW

AGILE & SCRUM

Ajit Singh

For information about this title or to order other books and/or electronic media, contact the publisher:

Ajit Singh
ajit_singh24@yahoo.com
http://www.ajitvoice.in

Library of Congress Control Number: (N/A)
ISBN: 9781099820311
Cover and Interior design: Ajit Singh.

Preface

"One of the first questions we ask ourselves for each of our project implementations is "Which development methodology should we use?" This is a topic that gets a lot of discussion as it's the way of organizing the work for the project and not as often misinterpreted about a style of project management or a specific technical approach. The two basic and most popular methodologies are:

1. Waterfall: which is known as the "traditional" approach, and

2. Agile: a specific type of Rapid Application Development and newer than Waterfall, but not that new, which is often implemented using Scrum. Both are usable, mature methodologies.
The concepts of agile development were introduced when programmers were experiencing different obstacles in building software in various aspects. The obsolete waterfall model became defective and was no more pure process in terms of developing software. Consequently new other development methods have been introduced to mitigate the defects.

The purpose of this book is to study different agile methods and find out the best one for software development. Each important agile method offers own practices, release planning methodology, sprint planning. They differ in sizes and principles. The purpose of this book is to attain knowledge about all these facts and understand the agile software development environment. Popular agile methods are analyzed and explained in the theory part of this book; where methods have been compared with each other.

The percentage of agile practice is booming. Software development organizations and teams no longer keep faith on traditional development methods. Waterfall method has become obsolete and not effective anymore in building large and complex projects. This book presents the reasons and benefits of agile practice and also demonstrates the top software development methods adopted by software development organizations.

At the end of this book the guide for Scrum implementation has been presented. Scrum is the most popular lightweight agile method for software development. The Scrum team and the role of Scrum Master have been discussed in detail. The Scrum events and artifacts reveal the key aspects of Scrum implementation.

Lately, Agile and especially Scrum have become more and more popular. A lot of people in higher management see the agile way of working as the key to success. But is this actually true? Have we found the silver bullet? Can every individual work in an agile way? If yes, does this mean that the team that he is part of will also adopt and use the agile way of working and thinking successfully?

All those questions triggered this handy textbook.

Ajit Singh

Contents

Section 3. Values of Agile Methods

Customer Collaboration over Contract Negotiation
Individuals and Interactions over processes and tools
Working Software over Comprehensive Documentation
Responding to Change over Following a Plan
The Principles for Agile Software development
Agile Software Engineering
Requirements
Architecture
Design
Construction
Testing
Types of Agile Methods and Descriptions
Scrum
Extreme Programming (XP)

Crystal
Feature Driven Development (FDD)
Adaptive Software Development (ASD)
Dynamic System Development Method (DSDM)
Comparison of Agile Methods
Advantages and Disadvantages of Different Agile Methods

Section 4. SCRUM Methodologies

Section 5. SCRUM Implementation

The Scrum Theory
The Scrum Team
The Product Owner
The Development Team
The Scrum Master
Scrum Events
The Sprint
The Sprint Planning Meeting
Daily Scrum
Sprint Review
Scrum Artifacts
Product Backlog
Sprint Backlog
Increment

Chapter 1 - Waterfall versus Agile

Waterfall Model design

The Waterfall Model was first Process Model to be introduced. It is also referred to as a linear-sequential life cycle model. It is very simple to understand and use. In a waterfall model, each phase must be completed before the next phase can begin and there is no overlapping in the phases.

In more details, waterfall approach was first SDLC (System Development Life Cycle) Model to be used widely in Software Engineering to ensure success of the project. In "The Waterfall" approach, the whole process of software development is divided into separate phases. In Waterfall model, typically, the outcome of one phase acts as the input for the next phase sequentially.

Following is a diagrammatic representation of different phases of waterfall model.

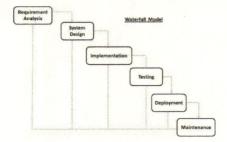

Figure 1: Waterfall software development life cycle model

Source: (Gingco, 2016)

The sequential phases in Waterfall model are:

Requirement Gathering and analysis: All possible requirements of the system to be developed are captured in this phase and documented in a requirement specification doc.

System Design: The requirement specifications from first phase are studied in this phase and system design is prepared. System Design helps in specifying hardware and system requirements and helps in defining overall system architecture.

Implementation: With inputs from system design, the system is first developed in small programs called units, which are integrated in the next phase. Each unit is developed and tested for its functionality which is referred to as Unit Testing.

Integration and Testing: All the units developed in the implementation phase are integrated into a system after testing of each unit. Post integration the entire system is tested for any faults and failures.

Deployment of system: Once the functional and non-functional testing is done, the product is deployed in the customer environment or released into the market.

Maintenance: There are some issues which come up in the client environment. To fix those issues patches are released. Also, to enhance the product some better versions are released. Maintenance is done to deliver these changes in the customer environment.

All these phases are cascaded to each other in which progress is flowing steadily downwards (like a waterfall) through the phases. The next phase is started only after the defined set of goals are achieved for previous phase and it is signed off, so the name "Waterfall Model". In this model phases do not overlap.

Every software developed is different and requires a suitable SDLC approach to be followed based on the internal and external factors. Some situations where the use of Waterfall model is most appropriate are:

1. Requirements are very well documented, clear and fixed.

2. Product definition is stable.

3. Technology is understood and is not dynamic. There are no ambiguous requirements.

4. Ample resources with required expertise are available to support the product. The project is short.

In conclusion, the main advantage of waterfall development is that it allows for departmentalization and control. A schedule can be set with deadlines for each stage of development and a product can proceed through the development process model phases one by one. Once an application is in the testing stage, it is very difficult to go back and change something that was not well-documented or thought upon in the concept stage.

Agile Methodologies

What Is Agile
Agile is a time boxed, iterative approach to software delivery that builds software incrementally from the start of the project, instead of trying to deliver it all at once near the end. It works by breaking projects down into little bits of user functionality called user stories, prioritizing them, and then continuously delivering them in short two week cycles called iterations (http://www.agilenutshell.com, 2017).

Figure 2: Agile Methodologies

Agile Methodologies are models used in the system development arena. The agile methodology has evolved in the mid-1990s as a part of reaction against traditional waterfall methods. That the Agile Methodologies were originating resulted from the use of the waterfall model were inflexible, slow, and inconsistent with the ways that software developers perform effective work. Agile development methods mark a return to development practice from early in the history of software development.

The use of the word agile in this context derives from the agile manifesto (http://leadinganswers.typepad.com/, 2017).

History: The Agile Manifesto

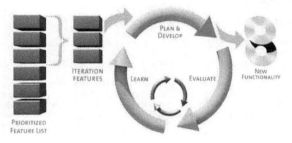

Figure 3: The Agile Manifesto (Self Drawn)

Methodologists are about delivering good products to customers by operating in an environment that does more than talk about "people as our most important asset" but "acts" as if people were the most important, and lose the word "asset".

The meeting at Snowbird was incubated at an earlier get together of Extreme Programming proponents, and a few "outsiders," organized by Kent Beck at the Rogue River Lodge in Oregon in the spring of 2000. At the Rogue River meeting attendees voiced support for a variety of "Light" methodologies, but nothing formal occurred. During 2000, several articles were written that referenced the category of "Light" or "Lightweight" processes. A number these articles referred to "Light methodologies, such as Extreme Programming, Adaptive Software Development, Crystal, and SCRUM". In conversations, no one really liked the moniker "Light", but it seemed to stick for the time being. In September 2000, Bob Martin from Object Mentor in Chicago, started the next meeting ball rolling with an email; "I'd like to convene a small (two day) conference in the January to February 2001 timeframe here in Chicago. The purpose of this conference is to get all the lightweight method leaders in one room. All of you are invited; and I'd be interested to know who else I should approach." Bob set up a Wiki site and the discussions raged. Early on, Alistair Cockburn weighed in with an epistle that identified the general disgruntlement with the word 'Light': "I don't mind the methodology being called light in weight, but I'm not sure I want to be referred to as a lightweight attending a lightweight methodologists meeting. It somehow sounds like a bunch of skinny, feebleminded lightweight people trying to remember what day it is." The fiercest debate was over location! There was serious concern about Chicago in wintertime—cold and nothing fun to do; Snowbird, Utah—cold, but fun things to do, at least for those who ski on their heads like Martin Fowler tried on day one; and Anguilla in the Caribbean—warm and fun, but time consuming to get to. In the end, Snowbird and skiing won out; however, a few people—like Ron Jeffries—want a warmer place next time.

I hope that my work together as the Agile Alliance helps others in our profession to think about software development, methodologies, and organizations, in new– more agile

– ways. If so, we've accomplished our goals." (http://agilemanifesto.org/principles.html)

The Core Principles of Agile

Without standards of excellence for agile, anyone can call anything agile. Over the years several myths have formed around Agile delivery. Here are some of the more popular ones.

Agile is a silver bullet:

You can fail just as spectacularly on an Agile project as you can be using any other traditional method. The difference to that is that You'll fail faster using Agile (due to the transparency and visibility it brings) but unfortunately, it's not a silver bullet or an excuse to stop thinking.

There's nothing inherently magical about Agile. It basically says Bring your development team and customer as close together as you can, give them what they need, and then get out of the way.

Agile is anti-documentation:

Where Agile pushes back on documentation is as a means of communication. Agile prefers face-to-face communication over relying on the written word. But isn't anti-documentation. Documentation gets treated like any other deliverable on an Agile project. It gets estimated, sized, and prioritized like any other user story.

Agile is anti-planning:

Agile is just anti-static planning. Users of Agile expect their plans to change and use tools like burndown charts to track and make these changes visible.

There's a lot of planning that goes on in Agile projects like daily planning, iteration planning meetings, sprint planning meetings, release planning.

Agile is undisciplined:

Agile is a very disciplined way of delivering software which requires a lot of hard work, courage, and discipline. With Agile you are obliged to:

Test

II. Get feedback.

III. Ship software regularly.

IV.   Be ready to change and update the plan.

Deliver bad news early.

Agile requires a lot of rework:

When it comes to rework you've got the rework of requirements (customers discovering what they really want) and the rework of the software (development teams discover better ways to design the software).

Both need to be balanced and tempered. Agile deals with this tension by empowering both sides with the power to iterate, so long as they work within the project's means. Burndown charts play in big role in tracking how Agile project are doing. Just as tools like the Agile Inception Deck make sure everyone is on the same page with regards to time and money (http://agilemanifesto.org/principles.html).

Agile is anti-architecture:

Agile created terms like YAGNI (You Aint Gonna Need It) to remind teams to keep things simple until proven otherwise.

That doesn't mean Agile teams stop thinking, or don't leverage previous experiences. It's mostly building the mind-set that the best way to build systems is to keep things simple, and only add the complexity when you need it.

Figure 4: Agile like YAGNI

Source: (Kourounakis, 2014)

Agile doesn't scale:

There is no easy way to magically coordinate, communicate, and keep large groups of people all moving in the same direction towards the same cause. It's hard work.

The one thing Agile does, is instead of looking for ways to scale up your project, look for ways to scale things down. In other words, if we know we are good at delivering with small, nimble, agile teams of ten, why don't we structure our work that way.

Agile Model Pros & Con

Pros:

Transparency: The customer has frequent and early opportunities to see the work being delivered, and to make decisions and changes throughout the

development project (from prioritizing features to iteration planning and review sessions to frequent software builds containing new features.).
Stakeholder Engagement: The customer gains a strong sense of ownership by

working extensively and directly with the project team throughout

the project. By involving the client in every step of the project, there is a high degree of collaboration between the client and project team, providing more opportunities for the team to truly understand the client's vision. Delivering working software early and frequently increases stakeholders' trust in the team's ability to deliver high-quality working software and encourages them to be more deeply engaged in the project

Early and Predictable Delivery: If time to market for a specific application is a greater concern than releasing a full feature set at initial launch, Agile can

more quickly produce a basic version of working software which can be built upon in successive iterations.

Improved Quality: By breaking down the project into manageable units, the project team can focus on high-quality development, testing, and

collaboration. Also, by producing frequent builds and conducting testing and reviews during each iteration, quality is improved by finding and fixing defects quickly and identifying expectation mismatches early.

Development is often more user-focused: Agile commonly uses user stories with business-focused acceptance criteria to define product features. By

focusing features on the needs of real users, each feature incrementally delivers value, not just an IT component. This also provides the opportunity to beta test software after each Sprint, gaining valuable feedback early in the project and providing the ability to make changes as needed.

Predictable Costs: Because each Sprint is a fixed duration, the cost is predictable and limited to the amount of work that can be performed by the

team in the fixed-schedule time box.

Cons:

Transparency: clients to understand that they are seeing a work in progress in exchange for this added benefit of transparency.

Agile works best when members of the development team are completely dedicated to the project.

Because Agile focuses on time-boxed delivery and frequent reprioritization, it's possible that some items set for delivery will not be completed within the

allotted timeframe. Additional sprints (beyond those initially planned) may be needed, adding to the project cost. In addition, customer involvement often leads to additional features requested throughout the project. Again, this can add to the overall time and cost of the implementation.

The close working relationships in an Agile project are easiest to manage when the team members are in the same physical space, which is not always possible.

However, there are a variety of ways to handle this issue, such as webcams, collaboration tools, etc.

The iterative nature of Agile development may lead to a frequent refactoring if the full scope of the system is not considered in the initial architecture and

design. Without this refactoring, the system can suffer from a reduction in overall quality. This becomes more pronounced in larger-scale implementations, or with systems that include a high level of integration.

Agile is a powerful tool for software development, not only providing benefits to the development team, but also providing a number of important business benefits to the client. Agile helps project teams deal with many of the most common project pitfalls (such as cost, schedule predictability and scope creep) in a more controlled manner. By reorganizing and re-envisioning the activities

involved in custom software development,
Agile achieves those same objectives in a leaner and more business-focused way.

In conclusion: What is being Agile?

Responding to change

Early feedback

Continuous improvement with inspection and adaptation

Reduced risk

Shorter development cycles and more frequent releases

Visible and transparent

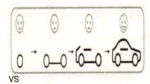 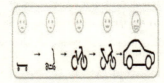

VS

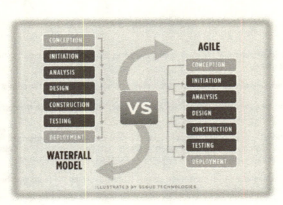

Figure 6: Software Development Estimation: Minimum Viable Product
Source: (Makarov, 2016)

Chapter 2 - Most commonly used Agile Methods & Practices

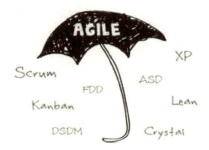

Introduction

The Agile Methodologies differ in the approaches of development and management they propose. (http://martinfowler.com/articles/newMethodology.html)

Some agile methods focus more extensively on project management and collaboration practices such as Scrum, Adaptive Software Development (ASD), and Lean Development. However, some agile methods concentrate heavily on software implementation practices such as Extreme Programming (XP), Agile Modelling (AM), and Feature-driven Development (FDD). At this book, we will focus only on Scrum and we will only give a short definition for the rest of methodologies.

Agile Methodologies

Adaptive software development (ASD)

Adaptive software development (ASD) is a software development embodies the principle that continuous adaptation of the process to the work at hand is the normal state of affairs. Adaptive software development replaces the traditional waterfall cycle with a repeating series of speculate, collaborate, and learn cycles. This dynamic cycle provides for continuous learning and adaptation to the emergent state of the project. The characteristics of an ASD life cycle are that it is mission focused, feature based, iterative, time boxed, risk driven, and change tolerant.

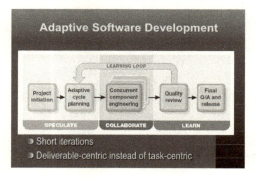

Figure 8:Adaptive software development

Source: (Virine & Trumper, 2007)

The word speculate refers to the paradox of planning – it is more likely to assume that all stakeholders are comparably wrong for certain aspects of the project's mission, while trying to define it. During speculation, the project is initiated and adaptive cycle planning is conducted. Adaptive cycle planning uses project initiation information—the customer's mission statement, project constraints (e.g., delivery dates or user descriptions), and basic requirements—to define the set of release cycles (software increments) that will be required for the project. Collaboration refers to the efforts for balancing the work based on predictable parts of the environment (planning and guiding them) and adapting to the uncertain surrounding mix of changes caused by various factors, such as technology, requirements, stakeholders, software vendors. The learning cycles, challenging all stakeholders, are based on the short iterations with design, build and testing. During these iterations the knowledge is gathered by making small mistakes based on false assumptions and correcting those mistakes, thus leading to greater experience mastery in the problem domain and eventually (Highsmith J. , 2000; Highsmith & Addison-Wesley, 2004)

"Messy, Exciting, and Anxiety-Ridden: Adaptive Software Development".

"Adaptive SD".

Agile Modelling

Agile modelling (AM) is a methodology for modelling and documenting software systems based on best practices. It is a collection of values and principles, that can be applied on an (agile) software development project. This methodology is more flexible than traditional modelling methods, making it a better fit in a fast changing environment (State of Agile Development Survey Results, 2011) . It is part of the agile software development tool kit.

Agile modelling is a supplement to other agile development methodologies such as Scrum, extreme programming (XP), and Rational Unified Process (RUP). It is explicitly included as part of the disciplined agile delivery (DAD) framework. As per 2011 stats, agile modelling accounted for 1% of all agile software development.[2]

• Agile modelling (AM) home page, effective practices for modelling and documentation

Agile Modeling Lifecycle

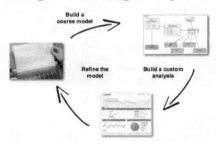

Figure 9: Agile Modeling Lifecycle

Source: (Nierstrasz, 2013)

Crystal Clear methods:

Crystal Clear is a member of the Crystal family of methodologies and is considered an example of an agile or lightweight methodology. (Cockburn)

Crystal Clear can be applied to teams of up to 6 or 8 co-located developers working on systems that are not life-critical. The Crystal family of methodologies focus on efficiency and habitability as components of project safety. Crystal Clear focuses on people, not processes or artifacts.

Crystal Clear requires the following properties:

Frequent delivery of usable code to users

Reflective improvement

Osmotic communication preferably by being co-located

Crystal Clear additionally includes these optional properties:
Personal safety

Focus

Easy access to expert users

Automated tests, configuration management, and frequent integration

Dynamic systems development method (DSDM):

Dynamic systems development method (DSDM) is an agile project delivery framework, primarily used as a software development method. (Richards, 2007) First released in 1994,

DSDM originally sought to provide some discipline to the rapid application development (RAD) method (Abrahamsson, 2003) . In 2007 DSDM became a generic approach to project management and solution delivery .DSDM is an iterative and incremental approach that embraces principles of Agile development, including continuous user/customer involvement.

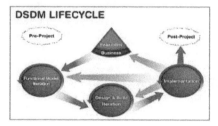

Figure 10:Dsdm lifecycle

DSDM fixes cost, quality and time at the outset and uses the MoSCoW2 prioritisation of scope into musts, shoulds, coulds and won't haves to adjust the project deliverable to meet the stated time constraint. DSDM is one of several Agile methods for developing software and non-IT solutions, and it forms a part of the Agile Alliance.

Values of Agile Methods

There are four major values of agile methods, and the values are: Individuals and interactions over processes and tools, collaboration of customer over contract negotiation, working software over comprehensive documentation, and responding to change over following a plan. The success of agile project depends on these values. (Rico et al. 2009, 7 – 8.)
Customer Collaboration over Contract Negotiation

The customers might not have the skills to perfectly specify the system but only they can tell what they want. Though it is hard to work with the customer but it's the reality of jobs.

It's important to have a contract with the customer, and having a concept of everyone's responsibilities and rights may form the base of that contract. Successful developers pay especial attention over their customers to find out what their customer's needs and they work closely with their customers. (Ambler 2002, 7.)

Individuals and Interactions over processes and tools

This means programmers are authorized to make their teams and manage themselves. This also means developers are enough competent on computer programming. The fact is; the job of programmer is to build computer software, so they are exceptionally skilled at it. Programmers can get guideline and support from processes and tools make effectiveness better. But all the processes and tools are useless and would not create any results when there is lacking of behavioral and technical skills among the developers. More importantly, this value means also programmers work together to find out a better solution of a complex problems which is not possible to solve by a single person. (Rico et al. 2009, 9.)

Working Software over Comprehensive Documentation

This means building working software is the primary goal of software development, not documentations. It is one of the highest priorities within agile methods. Customers pay for workable software, not for documentation. And this is the way to maximize the business value. (Rico et al. 2009, 9 – 10.)

Responding to Change over Following a Plan

This means being adaptable to alter. Develop software, test it and show it to the customer and change the plan if it is necessary; repeats the process until the customer is satisfied. Customer can change their priorities for different reasons. Moreover, technology changes over the time, there can be change in business environment. These have effects on software engineering. In software development the change is obvious. There should be balance between changing and planning. There should be opportunity to alter the project when situation demands; otherwise the project plan would be irrelevant. (Ambler 2002, 7.)

The Principles for Agile Software development

The members of the Agile Alliance defined their manifesto into a collection of twelve principles to help people get a sheer understanding of what agile software development is all about. These principles express all key features of agile development. A software development team can achieve knowledge about agile practices from these principles and the team must follows these principles while adopting agile as their software development method. These principles are: Our highest priority is to satisfy the customer through early and continuous delivery of valuable software products. Welcome changing requirements, even late in development. Agile processes harness change for the customer's competitive advantage. Deliver working software frequently, from a couple of weeks to a couple of months, with a preference to the shorter time scale. Business people and developers must work together daily throughout the project. Build projects around motivated individuals. Give them the environment and support they need, and trust them to get the job done. The most efficient and effective method of conveying information to and within a development team is face-to-face conversation. Working software is the primary measure of progress. Agile processes promote sustainable development. The sponsors, developers, and users should be able to maintain a constant pace indefinitely. Continuous attention to technical excellence and good design enhances agility. Simplicity—the art of maximizing the amount of work not done—is essential. The best architectures, requirements, and designs emerge from self-organizing teams. At regular intervals, the team reflects on how to become more effective, and then tunes and adjusts its behaviour accordingly. (Ambler 2002, 7 – 8.)

Agile Software Engineering

Agile software development harmonizes teamwork, customer collaboration, iterative development, and adaptability to build, operate and maintain new software products. Through flexible and adaptable development process which are quantifiable, systematic and disciplined, the agile software engineering is just-enough, right-sized and just-in-time to get the task done. Agile engineering varies a lot compared with obsolete waterfall model. Time boxed iteration and evolutionary software development which includes planning with continuous changing are the important features of agile engineering. Agile development process includes also evolutionary delivery system, which refers that the software is developed gradually with small portion at a time. Flexible and comfortable manner towards changes is the essential part of agile software engineering. (Rico et al. 2009, 49.)

There is no exact definition of agile methods, and all agile methods contain the same foundation. There are some specific practices which vary in every agile method. Basic practices like short time-boxed iterations with adaptive, evolutionary refinement of plans and goals are been shared by different agile methods. (Larman 2004, 25.)

Requirements

In term of software engineering, software requirements are known as the properties which must be revealed to solve a problem. Moreover, it is also a way of specifying, eliciting analyzing, and validating customer requirements. Software requirements specifications are a major component in traditional methods. (Rico et al. 2009, 50.)

Software requirements are treated as user stories in agile methods, that are simple, very short statements that describe software functions that customer needs to add business value. There is a process for estimating, writing, sorting, splitting, spiking, and determining the velocity of user stories. User stories can be sorted to prioritize their execution by risk or business value. Customer then can choose the scope of a release by selecting from user stories. The objective of requirements can be attained from user stories. Then user stories can be documented within automated workflow tools or on index cards. Collaboration between developers and customers is the most valuable part of user stories. Within agile methods, user stories are just-enough, right-size, and just-in-time software requirements to maximize business value. (Rico et al. 2009, 50.)

Architecture

Software architecture presents software subsystems and relationship among them. It's also a way of evaluating, specifying, selecting, and identifying an architectural pattern or style. Software architecture description is a vital component in traditional methods. In agile methods, software architecture is considered as system metaphors and it is narratives. It can be used to clarify the functions of the software products and how the products work. There is a way of developing metaphors. One of the objectives of initial iteration is to get a functional skeleton of the system as a whole. Developers build the complete architecture on the basis of user stories that are chosen by the customers. After choosing the user stories, developers and customers combine them into a simple narrative about the total functions and how the full system runs. In term of software engineering body of knowledge, system metaphors present the objective of software architecture. In agile methods, system metaphors are just-enough, right-sized, and just-in-time software architecture to maximize business value. (Rico et al. 2009, 50 – 51.)

Design

Software design is known as the interfaces, components, and characteristics. With the help of software design, it is possible to analyze quality, define software structure, apply design notations, and utilize software design methods. Software design description is an important component in traditional methods. (Rico et al. 2009, 51.)

In agile development, software design is known as simple design. It is a code design consists of small number of classes and methods which satisfy the user stories. The creation of simple design starts with a unit test for evaluating software methods. When the process of designing and implementation of just enough code is done for getting tests running, the process is iterated; that is, make some code and then remove the useless portion. There must be the reflections of all intentions in the code. Software design is a part of coding in agile methods but in traditional methods it is documentation. (Rico et al. 2009, 51.)

Construction

Software construction means the process of building working software. Moreover, it is also a process of writing code, unit testing, verification, integration testing, and debugging. Agile methods belongs practices for software construction, like pair programming, coding standards, and refactoring, collective ownership. Pair programming means that the two programmers are responsible for coding all software; coding standards refer to the programming language style guides; refactoring refers to the re- structure code whenever needs; and collective ownership refers that every programmers are authorized to alter the programming code whenever needs. (Rico et al. 2009, 51 – 52.)

After getting programming tasks, programmers estimate them, find a suitable partner, make unit tests, maintain style of codding standards, build simple code, and go for the test of the code. Pair programming, coding standards, refactoring, and collective ownership refer the objective of software construction. Software construction is considered as the least important activity in traditional methods, but in case of agile methods, a flexible layer of software developing discipline is held over software construction that makes sure effective software to be built in 14 to 30 day iterations. These types of practices are justenough, right-sized, and just-in-time software construction in agile development to maximize business value. (Rico et al. 2009, 52.)

Testing

In software engineering, software testing is the process to evaluate the function and quality of software. Moreover, software testing is the process of developing test plans, procedures, design, script, cases, and reports. Software testing is the major components in traditional methods which document the test levels, progression, conditions, procedures, data, environment and schedules. (Rico et al. 2009, 52.)

There are practices in agile methods for software testing, like continuous integration and test driven development, that are ways of creating unit tests before software coding and integrating all changes into the system baseline to verify them by automated frameworks. In term of software engineering body of knowledge, continuous integration and test driven development provide the objective of software testing. In agile development adaptable process, pair programming, and customer collaboration make a validation and verification life cycle. In agile development, continuous integration and test driven development are just-enough, right-sized, and just-in-time testing for maximizing business value. (Rico et al. 2009, 52 – 53.)

Types of Agile Methods and Descriptions

There are many types of agile methods. Each agile method has own distinction. They differ from sizes, practices, and flexibilities. Though they differ from each other, the main principles of all agile methods are almost same. All of these methods present the frameworks for developing effective software products. Here are the types and descriptions of most common agile methods in the following. (Rico et al. 2009, 25.)

Scrum

Origins of Scrum

Of historical interest is that Scrum was incubated at Easel Corporation in 1993 where I had just joined them as VP of Object Technology after spending 4 years as President of Object Databases, a startup surrounded by the MIT campus in a building that housed some of the first successful AI companies.

My mind was steeped in artificial intelligence, neural networks, and artificial life. If you read most of the resources on Luis Rocha's page on Evolutionary Systems and Artificial Life you can generate the same mind set:

http://informatics.indiana.edu/rocha/alife.html

I leased some of my space to a robotics professor at MIT, Rodney Brooks, for a company now known as IROBOT Corporation. Brooks was promoting his subsumption architecture where a bunch of independent dumb things were harnessed together so that feedback interactions made them smart, and sensors allowed them to use reality as an external database, rather than having an internal datastore.

Prof. Brooks viewed the old AI model of trying to create an internal model of reality and computing off that simulation was a failed AI strategy that had never worked and would never work. You cannot make a plan of reality because there are too many datapoints, too many interactions, and too many unforeseen side effects. This is most obviously true when you launch an autonomous robot into an unknown environment.

The woman I believe will one day be known as the primeval robot mother by future intelligent robots was also working in my offices giving these robots what looked like emotional behavior to an external observer. Conflicting lower level goals were harnessed to produce higher goal seeking behavior. These robots were running in and aroundmy desk during my daily work.

I asked IROBOT to bring a spider-like robot to an adult education course that I was running with my wife (the minister of a local Unitarian Church) where they laid the robot on the floor with eight or more dangling legs flopping loosely. Each leg segment had a microprocessor and there were multiple processors on its spine and so forth. They inserted a blank neural network chip into a side panel and turned it on.

The robot began flailing like an infant, then started wobbling and rolling upright, staggered until it could move forward, and then walked drunkenly across the room like a toddler. It was so humanlike in its response that it evoked the "Oh, isn't it cute!" response in all the women in the room. We had just watched the first robot learn how to walk.

That demo forever changed the way the people in that room thought about robots, people, and life even though most of them knew little about software or computers. (I believe the robot's name was Genghis Khan and he is now in the Smithsonian.) This concept of a harness to help coordinate via feedback loops, while having the feedback be reality based fro real data coming from the environment is central to human groups achieving higher level behavior than an yindividual could achieve on their own. Maximizing communication of essential information between group members actually powers up this higher-level behavior.

Around the same time, a seminal paper was published out of the Santa Fe Institute mathematically demonstrating that evolution proceeds most quickly, as a system is made flexible to the edge chaos. This demonstrated that confusion and struggle was essential to emerging peak performance (of people or software architectures which are journeys though an evolutionary design space) as was seen in the robot demo.

Scrum is the method first created by Jeff Sutherland in 1993, and it is the most common and used agile method in the world. There were two basic reasons for creation of scrum: Existing methods were not so effective, and a new method was necessary to make sure the project success. Scrum considers that there is a need of adaptable software development method because of unpredictable software development and ironclad project plans do not work. Eventually, to make plans successful and help real-world project, Scrum was created. Initially Scrum had three broad phases: Pre-sprint planning, Sprint, and Postsprint meeting. However, now a days Scrum has five major phases: Sprint planning meeting, Sprint, Daily stand-up meetings, Sprint review meetings, and Sprint retrospective meetings. (Rico et al. 2009, 25 – 26.)

Daily stand-up and retrospective meetings are the significant ideas which are responsible for rich interpersonal communication and process improvement. The use of Scrum is booming in software engineering, where 50% of software engineers prefer Scrum as their software engineering method. (Rico et al. 2009, 26.)

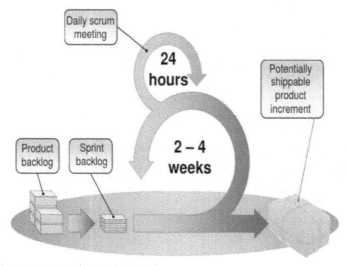

Graph 2: Scrum Process (Rico et al. 2009, 26.)

Two meetings are held before the start of each iteration or Sprint; where in the first meeting, stakeholders refine and re-prioritize the Product Backlog and Release Backlog. They select the goals for the next iteration in this meeting. The Scrum Team and the Product Owner meet in the second meeting, where the objective of this meeting is to determine how to achieve the request, and to make a Sprint Backlog of tasks to fulfil the goals. Another new planning cycle might occur in term of the failure of the estimated effort. Task is formed in 30-calendar iterations; where each is known as a Sprint. (Larman 2004, 117.)

The management and the Scrum Master neither manage the team in achieving iteration goals nor plan the order of tasks. The team is quite free and authorized to find their best process, and find their own way to solve problems.Same special questions are answered by the each team member during a meeting which is held in each workday at the same place and time.Tasks are fixed within a sprint. Management does not add extra works to the team during iteration. Uninterrupted focus is a special feature of Scrum. It is very rare that something is added, but in this case it is ideal to remove something else. (Larman 2004, 117 – 118.)

It is Scrum Masters duty to ensure that team is not interrupted by external parties with work requests. If it happens then removes them and makes deals with all political and external management issues. The Scrum Master works also to make sure that Scrum is applied, provides resources, removes reported blocks, and makes decisions when he/she is requested. During a meeting, if it reveals that someone is not completing work, and the team is careless about it then the Scrum Master takes proper initiatives to fix this issue. (Larman 2004, 118.)

Blocks reported at the Scrum meeting that need decisions by the Scrum Master are made forthwith, or within one hour. The reported blocks are ideally removed before the next Scrum Meeting. Only the Scrum Team can talk (the pigs) during the Scrum Meeting. Anybody else can attend the meeting if he/she wish but should keep quiet (the chickens) during the meeting. Client-driven adaptive planning is maintained in all iterations. Demo is shown to the external stakeholders at the end of the iteration when the product is workable.
The demo can't be shown in terms of ineffective product. (Larman 2004, 118 – 119.)
Scrum is a light framework for the environment; like dynamic and which changes continuously. In Scrum, several variables are taken into account when building software and planning the releases. New requirements must be considered when planning iterations as customer requirements change continuously. In the beginning of the project there are some important things to consider, like time frame, resources, and backup. Each Scrum team should be consisted with less than eight members but multiple teams may build a project and form the increment. Both in small projects and large projects Scrum is used with hundreds of programmers. Scrum teams work in a common project room, where they arrange their daily stand-up meetings. (Larman 2004, 111.)
There is no strict obligation to work in the same working room; it is possible to work in separate room also, but free communication is an essential part of the agile practice according to agile main principles. Eventually, the open-plan office is the appeasement selection for working space. In case of lacking of free common room, corridor can be used also for daily stand-up meetings. (Larman 2004, 112.)
There are three main phases in Scrum lifecycle; pre-game, development, and postgame/release. Pre-game includes two sub-phases: planning, and architecture. Expectations and vision are set in the planning phase. The initial product backlog which contains all prioritized requirements is made in planning phase. Moreover, in planning phase vision is written, items are estimated, and budget is made. (Larman 2004, 113.)
According to the items in the product backlog list, a high level design of the system is planned in the architecture phase. Initial plans for the content of the releases are done also in the architecture phase. (Coram and Bohner 2005.). The implementation of the system is ready for release in a series of thirty day iteration (Sprints) in development phase. Usually one process consists with around three to eight Sprints before the system is ready for release. Both daily Scrum and Sprint planning meeting are held in all iterations. (Larman 2004, 113.)
The termination of the release takes place in the post-game phase (release phase). The product backlog list is totally free from requirements and the product is quite ready for release. Release phase belongs marketing & sales, and training also. (Coram and Bohner 2005.)

Extreme programming (XP):

Extreme programming (XP) is a software development methodology which is intended to improve software quality and responsiveness to changing customer requirements. As a type of agile software development, (Human Centred Technology Workshop 2005) it advocates frequent "releases" in short development cycles, which is intended to improve productivity and introduce checkpoints at which new customer requirements can be adopted. (Design Patterns and Refactoring). Other elements of extreme programming include: programming in pairs or doing extensive code review, unit testing of all code, avoiding programming of features until they are actually needed, a flat management structure, code simplicity and clarity, expecting changes in the customer's requirements as time passes and the problem is better understood, and frequent communication with the customer and among programmers (Agile Alliance, 2001).

Extreme Programming (XP) at a Glance

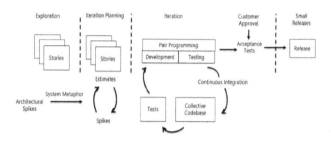

Figure 11: Extreme Programming (XP) at a Glance

Source: (Meier, 2014)

The methodology takes its name from the idea that the beneficial elements of traditional software engineering practices are taken to "extreme" levels. As an example, code reviews are considered a beneficial practice; taken to the extreme, code can be reviewed continuously, i.e. the practice of pair programming.

Feature-driven development (FDD):

Feature-driven development (FDD) is an iterative and incremental software development process. It is one of many lightweight or Agile methods for developing software. FDD blends industry-recognized best practices into a cohesive whole. These practices are all driven from a client-valued functionality (feature) perspective. Its main purpose is to deliver tangible, working software repeatedly in a timely manner.

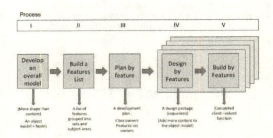

Figure 12: Feature-driven development (FDD)

Source: (Gayal & Ruhaim, 2014)
Lean software development:

Lean software development (LSD) is a translation of lean manufacturing and lean IT principles and practices to the software development domain. Adapted from the Toyota Production System, a pro-lean subculture is emerging from within the Agile community (Kanban, 2011).

Figure 13: Lean software development

Source: (Yasuhiro Monden, 1998)
Kanban

Kanban (看板?) (literally signboard or billboard in Japanese) is a scheduling system for lean manufacturing and just-in-time manufacturing (JIT) (Ohno, 1998). Kanban is an inventory-control system to control the supply chain. Taiichi Ohno, an industrial engineer at Toyota, developed Kanban to improve manufacturing efficiency. Kanban is one method to achieve JIT (Shingō, 1989).

Kanban became an effective tool to support running a production system and an excellent way to promote improvement. One of the main benefits of Kanban is to establish an upper limit to the work in process inventory, avoiding overloading of the manufacturing system.

Other systems with similar effect are for example CONWIP (Hopp, 2004). A systematic study of various configurations of Kanban systems, of which CONWIP is an important special case, can be found in Tayur (1993), among other papers (Tayur, 1993; Muckstadt & Tayur, 1995; Muckstadt & Tayur, 1995; Tayur, 1992; Schonberger, 2001).

LEAN METHODOLOGY

Figure 14: Albelli-payments team-Kanaban board (Self Drawn)

An English-language term that captures the meaning of the Japanese word, Kanban, is queue limiter; and the beneficial result is queue limitation (Waldner, 1992). Operationally, then, as process problems are dealt with, the queue limit (or maximum) should be reduced; for example, a former upper limit of five pieces is reduced to four, with queue time in the process reduced by 20 percent.

Scrum

Scrum is an iterative and incremental agile software development framework for managing product development (Verheyen, 2016). It defines "a flexible, holistic product development strategy where a development team works as a unit to reach a common goal", challenges assumptions of the "traditional, sequential approach" to product development, and enables teams to self-organize by encouraging physical co-location or close online collaboration of all team members, as well as daily face-to-face communication among all team members and disciplines involved (Takeuchi & Nonaka, 1986).

A key principle of Scrum is its recognition that during product development, the customers can change their minds about what they want and need (often called requirements volatility) (Henry & Henry, 1993), and that unpredicted challenges cannot be easily addressed in a traditional predictive or planned manner. As such, Scrum adopts an evidence-based empirical approach—accepting that the problem cannot be fully understood or defined, focusing instead on maximizing the team's ability to deliver quickly, to respond to emerging requirements and to adapt to evolving technologies and changes in market conditions (What is Scrum? An Agile Framework for Completing Complex Projects - Scrum Alliance. Scrum Alliance., 2016).

Figure 15: The Agile Scrum Framework at a glance

Source: (neonrain.com)

Scrumban

Scrumban is an Agile management methodology describing hybrids of Scrum and Kanban and was originally designed to transition from Scrum to Kanban. Today, Scrumban is a management framework that emerges when teams employ Scrum as their chosen way of working and use the Kanban Method as a lens through which to view, understand and continuously improve how they work (Pugh, 2011; Adzic, 2009).

Rapid application development (RAD)

Rapid application development (RAD) is both a general term used to refer to alternatives to the conventional waterfall model of software development as well as the name for James

Martin's approach to rapid development. In general, RAD approaches to software development put less emphasis on planning and more emphasis on process.

In contrast to the waterfall model, which calls for rigorously defined specification to be established prior to entering the development phase, RAD approaches emphasize adaptability and the necessity of adjusting requirements in response to knowledge gained as the project progresses. Prototypes are often used in addition to or sometimes even in place of design specifications.

RAD is especially well suited (although not limited to) developing software that is driven by user interface requirements. Graphical user interface builders are often called rapid application development tools.

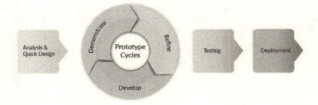

Figure 16: Prototype Cycles

Source : (www.wavemaker.com)

Agile practices

Agile development is supported by several concrete practices as well, covering areas like requirements, design, modelling, coding, testing, planning, risk management, process, quality, etc. Some notable agile practices include:

Acceptance test-driven development (ATDD)

Acceptance test–driven development (ATDD) is a development methodology based on communication between the business customers, the developers, and the testers

(Chelimsky, και συν., 2001). ATDD encompasses many of the same practices as specification by example (Adzic, How successful teams deliver the right software. Manning., 2011), behaviour-driven development (BDD), example-driven development (EDD), (Example Driven Design". , 2013) and support-driven development also called story test–driven development (SDD) ("Story Test-Driven Development", 2013). All these processes aid developers and testers in understanding the customer's needs prior to implementation and allow customers to be able to converse in their own domain language.ATDD is closely related to test-driven development (TDD). It differs by the emphasis on developer-tester-business customer collaboration. ATDD encompasses acceptance testing, but highlights writing acceptance tests before developers begin coding (Beck K. , 2002).

Behaviour-driven development (BDD)

Behaviour-driven development (BDD) is a software development process that emerged from test-driven development (TDD) (Behaviour-Driven Development, 2012) (Haring & deRuiter, 2011). Behaviour-driven development combines the general techniques and principles of TDD with ideas from domain-driven design and object-oriented analysis and design to provide software development and management teams with shared tools and a shared process to collaborate on software development (Solis & Wang, 2011).

Although BDD is principally an idea about how software development should be managed by both business interests and technical insight, the practice of BDD does assume the use of specialized software tools to support the development process (Bellware, 2008). Although these tools are often developed specifically for use in BDD projects, they be specialized forms of the tooling that supports test-driven development. The tools serve to add automation to the ubiquitous language that is a central theme of BDD.

BDD is largely facilitated using a simple domain-specific language (DSL) using natural language constructs (e.g., English-like sentences) that can express the behaviour and the expected outcomes. Test scripts have long been a popular application of DSLs with varying degrees of sophistication. BDD is considered an effective technical practice especially when the "problem space" of the business problem to solve is complex (Tharayil, 2016).

Business analyst designer method (BADM)

Business analysis is a study discipline of identifying business needs and determining solutions to business problems. Solutions often include a software-systems development component, but may also consist of process improvement, organizational change or strategic planning and policy development. The person who carries out this task is called a business analyst or BA (Kathleen, Vander, & Kimi, 2008).

Business analysts do not work solely on developing software systems. Those who attempt to do so run the risk of developing an incomplete solution ("Business Analysis Body of Knowledge v2.0", 2008).

Although there are different role definitions, depending upon the organization, there does seem to be an area of common ground where most business analysts work. The responsibilities appear to be:

3. To investigate business systems, taking a holistic view of the situation. This may include examining elements of the organisation structures and staff development issues as well as current processes and IT systems.

To evaluate actions to improve the operation of a business system. Again, this may require an examination of organisational structure and staff development needs, to ensure that they are in line with any proposed process redesign and IT system development.

To document the business requirements for the IT system support using appropriate documentation standards.

In line with this, the core business analyst role could be defined as an internal consultancy role that has the responsibility for investigating business situations, identifying and evaluating options for improving business systems, defining requirements and ensuring the effective use of information systems in meeting the needs of the business (Alternaltive

definition of Business Analysis from BCS ISEB. , 2008).

Cross-functional team

A cross-functional team is a group of people with different functional expertise working toward a common goal (Krajewski & Ritzman, 2005). It may include people from finance, marketing, operations, and human resources departments. Typically, it includes employees from all levels of an organization. Members may also come from outside an organization (in particular: from suppliers, key customers, or consultants).Cross-functional teams often function as self-directed teams assigned to a specific task which calls for the input and expertise of numerous departments. Assigning a task to a team composed of multi-disciplinary individuals increases the level of creativity. Each member offers an alternative perspective to the problem and potential solution to the task. In business today, innovation is a leading competitive advantage and cross-functional teams promote innovation through a creative collaboration process. Members of a cross-functional team must be well versed in multi-tasking as they are simultaneously responsible for their cross-functional team duties as well as their normal day-to-day work tasks.

Some studyers have viewed cross-functional interactions as cooperative or competitive in nature, while others have argued that organization's functional areas are often forced to compete and cooperate simultaneously with one another ("coopetition") and it is critical to understand how these complex relationships interplay and affect firm performance (Luo, Slotegraaf, & Xing, 2006).

Decision making within a team may depend on consensus, but often is led by a manager/coach/team leader. Leadership can be a significant challenge with cross-functional teams. Leaders are charged with the task of directing team members of various disciplines. They must transform different variations of input into one cohesive final output. Cross-functional teams can be likened to the board of directors of a company. A group of qualified individuals of various backgrounds and disciplines are assembled to collaborate in an efficient manner to improve the organization or solve a problem.

Some organizations are built around cross-functional workflows by having reporting lines to multiple managers. This type of management is called matrix management, and such organizations are often called matrix organizations.

Continuous integration (CI):

In software engineering, continuous integration (CI) is the practice of merging all developer working copies to a shared mainline several times a day. Grady Booch first named and proposed CI in his 1991 method, [1] although he did not advocate integrating several times a day (Booch, 1991).

Domain-driven design (DDD)

Domain-driven design (DDD) is an approach to software development for complex needs by connecting the implementation to an evolving model. [1] The premise of domain-driven design is the following:

i.placing the project's primary focus on the core domain and domain logic; ii.basing complex designs on a model of the domain;

iii.initiating a creative collaboration between technical and domain experts to iteratively refine a conceptual model that addresses domain problems (http://dddcommunity.org , 2017). 2.3.7 Pair programming

Pair programming is an agile software development technique in which two programmers work together at one workstation. One, the driver, writes code while the other, the observer or navigator, reviews each line of code as it is typed in. The two programmers switch roles frequently (Ramsey, Bourque, & Dupuis, 2001).

While reviewing, the observer also considers the "strategic" direction of the work, coming up with ideas for improvements and likely future problems to address. This frees the driver to focus all his or her attention on the "tactical" aspects of completing the current task, using the observer as a safety net and guide.

Planning poker

Planning poker, also called Scrum poker, is a consensus-based, gamified technique for estimating, mostly used to estimate effort or relative size of development goals in software development. In planning poker, members of the group make estimates by playing numbered cards face-down to the table, instead of speaking them aloud. The cards are revealed, and the estimates are then discussed. By hiding the figures in this way, the group can avoid the cognitive bias of anchoring, where the first number spoken aloud sets a precedent for subsequent estimates (Cohn, "Agile Estimating and Planning". Mountain Goat Software., 2005).

It is most commonly used in agile software development, in Scrum and Extreme Programming.

The method was first defined and named by James Grenning in 2002 and later popularized by Mike Cohn in the book Agile Estimating and Planning, whose company trade marked the term ("Planning poker - Trademark, , 2008) and a digital online tool (Cohn, 2016).

Refactoring

Code refactoring is the process of restructuring existing computer code—changing the factoring—without changing its external behaviour. Refactoring improves non-functional attributes of the software. Advantages include improved code readability and reduced complexity. These can improve source-code maintainability and create a more expressive internal architecture or object model to improve extensibility. Typically, refactoring applies a series of standardised basic micro-refactoring's, each of which is (usually) a tiny change in a computer program's source code that either preserves the behaviour of the software, or at least does not modify its conformance to functional requirements. Many development environments provide automated support for performing the mechanical aspects of these basic refactoring's. If done extremely well, code refactoring may also resolve hidden, dormant, or undiscovered computer bugs or vulnerabilities in the system by simplifying the underlying logic and eliminating unnecessary levels of complexity. If done poorly it may fail the requirement that external functionality not be changed, introduce new bugs, or both.

By continuously improving the design of code, we make it easier and easier to work with. This is in sharp contrast to what typically happens: little refactoring and a great deal of attention paid to expediently adding new features. If you get into the hygienic habit ofrefactoring continuously, you'll find that it is easier to extend and maintain code (Kerievsky, 2004).

Test-driven development (TDD)

Test-driven development (TDD) is a software development process that relies on the repetition of a very short development cycle: requirements are turned into very specific test cases, then the software is improved to pass the new tests, only. This is opposed to software development that allows software to be added that is not proven to meet requirements.

Kent Beck, who is credited with having developed or 'rediscovered' (Kent, 2012) the technique, stated in 2003 that TDD encourages simple designs and inspires confidence (Beck, 2003).

Test-driven development is related to the test-first programming concepts of extreme programming, begun in 1999 (Lee, 2001), but more recently has created more general interest in its own right (Newkirk & Vorontsov, 2004).

Programmers also apply the concept to improving and debugging legacy code developed with older techniques (Feathers, 2004).

User story

In software development and product management, a user story is a description consisting of one or more sentences in the everyday or business language of the end user or user of a system that captures what a user does or needs to do as part of his or her job function. User stories are used with agile software development methodologies as the basis for defining the functions a business system must provide, and to facilitate requirements management. It captures the "who", "what" and "why" of a requirement in a simple, concise way, often limited in detail by what can be hand-written on a small paper notecard.

A user story encapsulates the action of one function making it possible for software developers to create a vertical slice of their work.

Story-driven modelling

Story-driven modelling is an Object-oriented modeling technique. Other forms of Object-oriented modeling focus on class diagrams (Diethelm, Geiger, & Zündorf, 2004). Class diagrams describe the static structure of a program, i.e. the building blocks of a program and how they relate to each other (Van Gorp, 2008; Eickhoff, Geiger, Hahn, & Zündorf 2012). Class diagrams also model data structures, but with an emphasis on rather abstract concepts like types and type features (Norbisrath & Ulrich, 2013) (Zündorf, Schürr, & Winter, 1999; Ryser & Glinz, 2000).

Retrospective

An Agile retrospective is a meeting that's held at the end of an iteration in Agile software development (ASD). During the retrospective, the team reflects on what happened in the iteration and identifies actions for improvement going forward. Each member of the team members answers the following questions:

What worked well for us?

What did not work well for us?

What actions can we take to improve our process going forward?

The Agile retrospective can be thought of as a "lessons learned" meeting. The team reflects on how everything went and then decides what changes they want to make in the next iteration. The retrospective is team-driven, and team members should decide together how the meetings will be run and how decisions will be made about improvements.

Velocity tracking

Velocity is a capacity planning tool sometimes used in agile software development. Velocity tracking is the act of measuring said velocity. The velocity is calculated by counting the number of units of work completed in a certain interval, the length of which is determined at the start of the project ("Velocity:Measuring and Planning an Agile Project", 2010).

User Story Mapping

Story mapping consists of ordering user stories along two independent dimensions. The "map" arranges user activities along the horizontal axis in rough order of priority (or "the order in which you would describe activities to explain the behaviour of the system"). Down the vertical axis, it represents increasing sophistication of the implementation.

Given a story map so arranged, the first horizontal row represents a "walking skeleton", a barebones but usable version of the product. Working through successive rows fleshes out the product with additional functionality.

More Practices:

Requirements
Product Vision
        Product Backlog

                    Use Cases

                    Personas

Design
Emergent Design / Evolutionary Design

Design by Contract

System Metaphor

Construction
Coding Style / Coding Guidelines / Coding Standard

Collective Code Ownership

Daily Builds / Automated Builds

Software Metrics / Code Metrics & Analysis

Source Control / Version Control

Issue Tracking / Bug Tracking

Frequent Delivery / Frequent Releases

Testing - Unit Testing
Smoke Testing / Build Verification Test

Integration Testing

System Testing

Test Automation

Acceptance Criteria / Acceptance Testing

Process
Timeboxing / Fixed Sprints / Fixed Iteration Length

Sprint Backlog

Task Board

Definition of Done

Daily Stand-up Meeting / Daily Scrum

Sprint Review / Iteration Demo

Root Cause Analysis / 5 Whys

Burn Down Charts

Big Visible Charts

Organization
Small Team

Self-Organizing Team

Sitting Together / Common Workspace

Sustainable Pace

Move People Around

The Agile Alliance has provided a comprehensive online guide to applying agile these and other practices (http://agilemanifesto.org/principles.html).
Chapter 3 - Extreme Programming (XP)

Extreme Programming was developed by Kent Beck and his team of 20 developers including Ron Jeffries and Martin Fowler at Chrysler in around 1996. It was created to manage a failing payroll system project at Chrysler. Its initial practices were consisted with just-in-time evolution, aggressiveness, self-chosen tasks, communication, and modeldriven development. Its key practices extended later into 13 practices that belonged onsite customers, test-driven development, pair programming, and open workspaces; however, in today, Extreme Programming has over 28 practices and rules for planning, designing, coding, and testing. XP achieved significant public recognition 1999. (Rico et al. 2009, 27.)

Extreme Programming is founded on 4 values; communication, simplicity, feedback, and courage. The main focuses of XP are on skillful development practices, collaboration, and quick and early software creation. (Larman 2004, 137.)

Extreme Programming Project

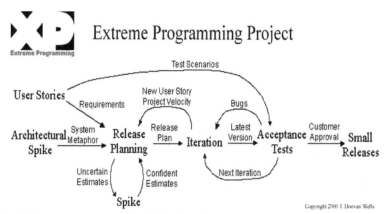

Test Scenarios

User Stories — Requirements — New User Story / Project Velocity — Bugs

Architectural Spike — System Metaphor — Release Planning — Release Plan — Iteration — Latest Version — Acceptance Tests — Customer Approval — Small Releases

Uncertain Estimates — Confident Estimates — Next Iteration

Spike

Graph 3: Extreme programming life cycle (Wells 1999)

All the contributors from one team sit together where team must include a business representative (Customer). The responsibilities of the customer are to provide requirements, set the priorities and steer the project. Programmers and testers are the other possible team members. Customer can get the help from analysts to define the requirements. Moreover, there might be a coach and the jobs of the coach are to help the team keep on the track and facilitate the process. The manager manages external communication, coordinates activities, and provides resources. The best teams have no specialists, just only general contributors with special skills. (Jeffries 2011.)

Extreme programming addresses two key questions in software engineering: predicting what will be executed by the due date, and determining what to do next. Planning games refers a set of rules and moves that might be utilized for simplifying the release planning process. It's customer who defines one or more automated acceptance test to demonstrate that the system is working. The team makes the tests and apply them to judge to themselves and to the customer, that the system is executed correctly. (Jeffries 2011.)

The team releases workable and tested software on every iteration. Software is visible, and at the end of iteration, software is given to customer. The customer can use that software for any purpose. Extreme programming teams develop software on the basis of simple design; though it is simple in design but adequate. The XP team makes the design in such a way so that it suits with the system that works here and now. (Jeffries 2011.)

In Extreme Programming, software is developed by two programmers who sit side by side at the same machine. This process makes sure that the code is reviewed by at least one other programmer. This makes the design, testing, and code much better. Every time any programmer releases any code to the repository every programmer tests are run perfectly. Programmer gets quick feedback in this way. In Extreme Programming method, _Refactoring' is a process which is followed to improve the design continuously. The duplications in coding are avoided and _cohesion' of the code is enhanced in refactoring process. Refactoring is strongly supported by comprehensive testing to make sure that nothing is broken. (Jeffries 2011.)

Throughout the development, the Extreme Programming teams keep the system quite integrated. The system is never far from a production state in this way. On an Extreme Programming project, any pair of programmers can improve any code at any time. In this way, all the code gets the benefit of many people's attention; as a result, code quality increases and it reduces the possibility of defective code. (Jeffries 2011.)

XP teams maintain a common coding standard system. Eventually all the code in the system looks like that it has been coded by a single individual who is very competent. XP teams form a common vision of how the program works; this is known as ̩metaphor'. In Extreme Programming, team members work hard at a pace that they can go along with for the time being. (Jeffries 2011.)

Extreme Programming is best suited with small and medium sized teams which consist with around three to twenty project members in a team. Communication and coordination between the team members is an essential part of Extreme Programming; hence, wide physical distance among the project members is not allowed. (Larman 2004, 142.)

In the Exploration phase, customer prepares the story cards (features) where they specify the requirements that would be included in the first release. Project team introduce themselves in the Exploration phase, where they present the technology and practices that would be used in project. The prototype of the system can be built also in this phase. The stories that are written by the customer are set into the priority order in the Planning phase. An agreement of the schedule and the content of the first release are made also in this phase. (Larman 2004, 142.)

The Iteration to release phase belongs several iteration before the first release. Each iteration needs one to four weeks to be executed. A system with the architecture of the full system is built in the first iteration. Functional tests that are made by the customer are run at the end of the every iteration. The system is ready for the production after the last iteration. (Coram and Bohner 2005.)

In Productionizing phase, more performance checks and tests are done before the system is ready to release. There might be new list of changes what might still be included in the ongoing release. The suggestions and ideas that are postponed are documented for later execution. (Coram and Bohner 2005.)

In Extreme Programming, system development and producing new iterations happens simultaneously. Support for the customer is given in the Maintenance phase. The Death phase takes place when all the stories are implemented and the customer does not have any stories to be executed. The documentation of the system is written and there is no more change in system architecture and code. (Coram and Bohner 2005.)

Crystal
The object-oriented programming method Crystal is created by Alistair Cockburn at IBM in 1991. Crystal Method is like a family that consists with 20 distinct agile methods, which are depicted by a two-dimensional grid. Essential memory, imagine life, discretionary money, and comfort on the y-axis and clear, yellow, orange, red, and maroon on the x-axis. There are seven broad stages of Crystal Methods: project cycle, delivery cycle, iteration cycle, integration cycle, week and day, development episode, and reflection about the process. (Rico et al. 2009, 31.)
Crystal Methods is quite a large agile method which consists with five strategies, seven properties, eight roles, nine techniques, and 25 documents. The latest version of this method is a composite of practices from other kind of agile methods. For example, information radiators of Crystal came from Scrum and Extreme Programming, and its burn charts, daily stand-ups, and reflection are from Scrum programming, and its iteration, release plan and side-by-side programming are from Extreme Programming. (Rico et al. 2009, 31-32.)

Crystal method developed with collected software development methodologies, which are communication-centric, people focused, ultra-light and highly tolerant. There are three properties which are central to every Crystal methodology: frequent delivery, reflective improvement, and close communication. (Schuh 2005, 30.)

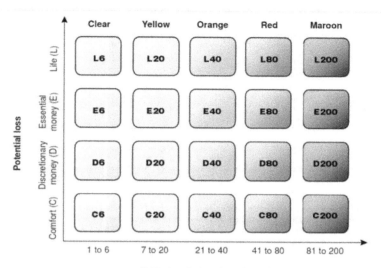

Project scale (number of people)

Graph 4: Crystal Methods (Rico et al. 2009, 32.)

Crystal methodologies have been catalogued on the basis of project size and criticality. Project size is determined by the member of the team and it is marked by the colour; as the darker the colour, the heavier the methodology. Criticality is marked by letter; for example, C: Comfort, D: Discretionary money, E: Essential money, and L: Life. According to the
Crystal, as the team becomes larger, a heavier methodology is needed. (Schuh 2005, 31.)

In Crystal methods, incremental development cycles are used and its lengths are not more than four months, however, the recommended lengths are one to three months. There is no definition in Crystal methodologies that which tools, work products, and development practices would be used in the project. Eventually, practices can be adopted from Scrum of Extreme Programming. (Schuh 2005, 33.)

Crystal Orange, Crystal Clear, and Crystal Orange Web are the three main Crystal methodologies that have been constructed. But in practice, only Crystal Orange and Crystal Clear have been constructed and used among these three main methodologies. Crystal Clear is for small project where each team consists with up to eight members who work in the same area. And Crystal Orange is for medium sized projects with 10 to 40 members. (Schuh 2005, 32.)

Policy standards of Crystal Clear and Crystal Orange are, every two to three months, software is delivered incrementally and regularly; progress is tracked by milestones based on software deliveries and key decisions rather than written documents; automated regression testing of application functionality; direct user involvement in the project; two user viewing per release; as upstream is ―stable enough to review‖, downstream activities are ready to start; and at the beginning and middle of each increment, product-and methodology-tuning are held. (Cockburn 2002.)

Within a time frame of two to three months, incremental delivery occurs in Crystal Clear; where in terms of Crystal Orange, the duration of the incremental delivery can be maximum four months. However, in case of delayed delivery, the development teams must negotiate with the customer and avoid less important tasks. (Schuh 2005, 32-34.)

Feature Driven Development (FDD)

Jeff De Luca and Peter Coad developed Feature Driven Development method in 1997 to save a failed banking project in Singapore. Feature Driven Development emphasizes on iterative development, quality and effective software, as well as an adaptable and flexible project management system. FDD consists with five broad phases: develop an overall model, build a features list, making plan by feature, design by feature, and build by feature. (Rico et al. 2009, 30 – 31.)

Feature Driven Development does not focus on entire software development process, its focus is on building phases and design. The agile team can adopt one or more practices from eight main practices of FDD; however by taking all eight practices in use, the best profit can be achieved. (Schuh 2005, 26.)

An overall roadmap to be built for the system. The roadmap is a composed of high-level diagrams that refer the relationships between sequence and class diagrams. Common foundation is maintained to all agile methodologies. Each class is assigned to a particular developer. It is just opposite of Extreme Programming's collective ownership. Due to the involvement of features with more than one class, to design and development in FDD feature teams are the common approach. Attention is paid on the identification of faults. Full system is developed at regular intervals in FDD. Throughout the lifetime of the project; the code, design, analysis, and testing artefacts are to be versioned and stored.
Regular and apprehensible updates of status are maintained in FDD. (Schuh 2005, 26.)
Feature Driven Development is consisted with five sequential processes (figure 5). The system is designed and developed completely during these processes. Usually an iteration of a feature needs one to three week period of task for the team. (Ambler 2005.)

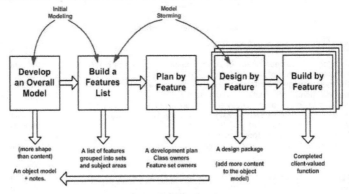

Graph 5: The FDD project lifecycle (Ambler 2005.)

Modelling at FDD is collaborative and time-boxed. Small groups create the domain model in details and then present for peers to review. It is expected that a suggested model or potentially a combination of them would then be used for each area of the domain. Then they will be merged over the time to develop an overall model. (Lawton 2015.)

A list of features is created on the basis of the knowledge that is gained during the modelling process. The list is created by dividing domains into subject fields that hold information on business activities. Some steps are followed for each business activity and these steps represent a categorised list of features. The form of expression of the features is: ─action, result, object‖. It is hoped that it will not take more than two weeks to complete; but they should be divided into smaller sections if it takes more than two weeks. (Lawton 2015.)

Once the feature list has been created, the following process involves assigning the different feature sets to the developers. Developers the build a design package for each feature with a chief developer selecting a group of features that should be built within a two week period. While refining the model, the chief developer would create diagrams in details for each feature. After completing this, prologues are developed and a design inspection is carried out. Once the design inspections are done, designers make a plan of activities for each feature and create the code for their respective classes. The feature is pushed to the main build when the inspection is made and a unit test carried out. (Lawton 2015.)

Adaptive Software Development (ASD)

Adaptive Software Development is focused at the project management level and its relationship with the organization it serves. Developers encounter problems in building large and complex systems; ASD emphasizes on those problems. In Adaptive Software Development, a dynamic Speculate-Collaborate-Learn lifecycle replaces the static PlanDesign-Build lifecycle. ASD project is handled with in cycle. There are three phases in each cycle (Figure 6): speculate, collaborate, and learn. (Schuh 2005, 36.)

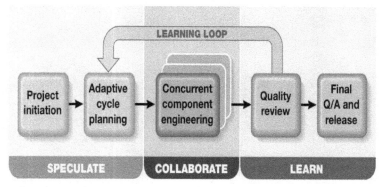

Graph 6: Adaptive Software Development lifecycle (Highsmith 2000.)

Speculate phase includes seven steps: conduct the project initial phase, determine the project time-box, determine the optimal number of cycles and the time-box for each cycle, create an objective statement for each cycle, allot primary components to cycles, assign technology and support components to cycles, and develop a project task list. (Highsmith 2000, 26.)

Delivering the working component is the purpose of Collaborate phase. In Adaptive Software development the main focus goes on the collaboration across the project team. For adopting collaboration within a project, there is no particular procedure recommendation from ASD. It is possible to adopt collaboration practices from Extreme Programming method. For example, for small teams; collective code ownership and pair programming are the suitable practices. (Highsmith 2000, 27.)

The main purpose of the Learn phase is feedback giving. There must have a review after ending of each iteration. The facts that take place in the review are: delivery teams' functions and practices utilized by the team, project status, and the quality of result of customers and technical point of view. (Highsmit 2000, 27.)

Adaptive Software Development life cycle has six characteristics. Mission focused: all the functions and tasks in every development cycle must be according to the ultimate project mission. Featured based: building activities are not set to task-oriented. Focus goes to building effective software by developing the system a small piece at a time. Iterative: according to the feedback from customers, components are developed over several iterative cycles. Time-boxed: project teams set their activities and functions according to the deadline of release. Project teams work hard to maintain the time frame. Risk driven: highrisk items should be developed as soon as possible. Change tolerant: programmers would constantly assess whether the items they have built are probably to alter. (Orr 2001, 175.)

Dynamic System Development Method (DSDM)

Dynamic System Development Method was created in 1993 by a British consortium of 16 academic and industry organizations. In UK, it is very popular for Rapid Application Development approach. At the beginning DSDM was consisted with three critical success factors: communication between end users and programmers, highly efficient programmers, and flexible customer requirements. Dynamic System Development method focuses on product versus process, integrated configuration management, fulfilling toppriority customer needs, and testing. (Rico et al. 2009, 27.)

In feasibility study stage of DSDM, it is determined that if Dynamic System Development method is suitable for the project. Technical feasibility of the project is evaluated also. Business process flows are assessed in business study stage. Development of functional models of the components takes place in functional model iteration stage. Prototypes are produced iteratively until quality products can be developed. The prototype is fleshed out and tested in system design and build iteration stage. In implementation stage, prototypes are applied to development and transferred into production. (Rico et al. 2009, 27 – 30.)

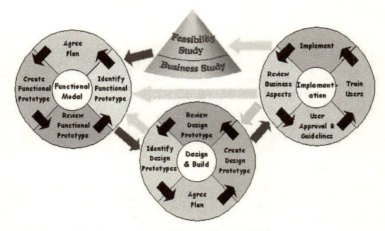

Graph 7: The DSDM Development Process (Clifton and Dunlap 2003.)

The people for whom the product is going to build must be involved with the development process. This is an important fact which leads the team to develop effective products. In DSDM, project teams are authorized to take instant decisions to make the project successful. Dynamic System Development Method focuses on frequent release. At the crucial stages of the product development, frequent releases allow for user input. They make sure that the product is ready to be released quickly at all times. (Clifton and Dunlap 2003.)

One of the important keys to DSDM's success is incremental product development process. It helps to break the bigger task into smaller task which makes the complex task easy. The most prioritized features and functionalities are developed as early as possible. It might need to change the project concerning issues at any stage of the project. The ultimate project aspects might not match with the project aspects it was before. Hence Dynamic System Development Method emphasizes on having opportunity for change in development cycle. (Clifton and Dunlap 2003.)

High level initial requirements are been executed in the initial stage of the project. Testing is made after each iteration that ensures the working product. Collaboration and team cooperation is the main strength of DSDM. It is essential for the success of the project. Not only the project team, but all involved parties must cooperate to achieve the business objective. (Clifton and Dunlap 2003.)

Comparison of Agile Methods

Method	Collaboration	Teamwork	Working software	Adaptability
Crystal	• Interaction design	• Daily standups	• Frequent delivery	• Blitz planning
Scrum	• Sprint reviews	• Daily standups	• 30-day sprints	• Sprint planning
DSDM	• User involvement	• Daily meetings	• Iterations	• Feasibility study
FDD	• Domain walkthrough	• Feature teams	• Feature build	• Feature planning
XP	• Onsite customers	• Pair programming	• 14-day iterations	• Release planning

Graph 8: Comparison of practices of different agile methods (Rico et al. 2009, 68.)

It is very important to choose an ideal agile method for a particular project. There are many lower-level practices in all agile methods practice lists. Agile methods belong some traditional practices like, risk management, inspections, configuration management, objectoriented design, prototyping, retrospectives. Programmers like to combine various agile practices from different agile methods and apply them in their project; because it is extremely hard to get all necessary practices from any particular agile method. The complexity, project length, resources, susceptibility to risk, stability of the requirements give variation to the projects. So if it needs to adopt some other agile methods in the middle of the project then it could create confusing atmosphere in the team. Hence, project teams must choose the perfect one or combine the best practices from different agile methods before starting a project. The following graphs demonstrate a short comparison of practices of different agile methods (Graph 8), and the pros and cons of different agile methods (Graph 9) (Rico et al. 2009, 67 – 69.):

Method	Pro	Con
Crystal	• Scalable family of practices • Collection of agile methods practices • Support for code reviews and inspections	• Amalgamation of agile methods practices • Traditional requirements methodology • Resembles traditional methodology
Scrum	• Adaptable planning framework • Adaptable requirements model • Emphasis on self-organizing teams	• No code reviews or inspections • No comprehensive testing methodology • Few customer interactions and automation
DSDM	• Strong customer involvement • Use of empowered project teams • Some support for iterative development	• Spinoff of Rapid Application Development • Resembles traditional methodologies • Weak iterative development model
FDD	• Semi-adaptable planning framework • Support for iterative development cycles • Support for code reviews and inspections	• Traditional requirements model • Significant up-front architecture and design • Few customer interactions and automation
XP	• Adaptable planning framework • Adaptable requirements model • Comprehensive testing methodology	• No code reviews or inspections • No support for virtual distributed teams • Viewed as a set of rules rather than tools

Graph 9: Pros and cons of different agile methods (Rico et al. 2009, 69):
Advantages and Disadvantages of Different Agile Methods

Scrum is a light process framework; it is possible to combine this method with process and practices from other detailed defined methods like Extreme Programming. The core of this method is self-organized team and teams strive hard to achieve the goals. There is no programming practices definition of Scrum for the implementation phase, but Scrum defines the expectations from the team and basic practices for the team in order to attain the goals. One of the important practices of Scrum is 15 minute daily start-up meeting, where team members answer the same accurately defined questions. It draws good impact on the team work and self-organization raises the motivation level. (Rico et al. 2009, 69 – 73.)

In Scrum all alteration are denied after the sprint requirements have been explained at the initial period of each sprint. It is good for the team as it ensures some time to execute all the works needed to finish the sprint requirement list. Sprint of one month may cause unacceptable delay, if customer is demanding a prompt solution for specific problem. Actual worst case delay may be then close to two months before the solution is seen in release. Scrum splits the problem into small pieces that are easily manageable for the team. (Rico et al. 2009, 69 – 73.)

One of the major advantage of Extreme Programming is it is enriched with wide range of information sources and it is widely used agile method. The actual management and programming practices are more detailed defined in Extreme Programming than to Scrum. Moreover, the process of iterations and frequent builds are well-arranged in Extreme Programming. The negative site of XP is on-site customer requirement is not possible to fulfil as Extreme Programming is applicable for small teams that are consisted with 5 – 10 programmers only. (Rico et al. 2009, 69 – 73.)

In Extreme Programming, developers are allowed to introduce new requirements and issues on the fly, which is effective in some situations to take quick steps to customer needs. The number of format meetings is reduced, and it is an effective way to share information through daily stand-up meetings. Extreme Programming is somewhat freeformed. (Rico et al. 2009, 69 – 73.)

Through reducing the amount of documentation, Extreme Programming increases production efficiency. It could be regarded either good or bad thing. In this way the product may be ready quickly but the product would be delivered to customer without updated documentation. Extreme Programming provides many use full practices but most often it is not possible to get a complete solution for a project through that practices. (Rico et al. 2009, 69 – 73.)

Crystal does not define any particular practices and tools for the project, but those could be adopted from other methods. Crystal has various type of process for small and large project, as a result finding suitable methodology is easy in here. The type Crystal clear is for small group consisted with maximum six programmers, and it needs a shared office space. However, for a medium-sized project and project team Crystal Orange is suitable. Crystal Orange defines effective communication between the team members. Each team working in the project should have a test engineer as testing is considered as integral part of the development. However, Crystal is not widely used method and it resembles with traditional methodology. And it is the amalgamation of different agile practices. (Rico et al. 2009, 69 – 73.)

Feature Driven Development defines model centric design which could create some impact on new starting team, and especially continuing old projects with no existing models. Individual code ownership is the weakest practice of Feature Driven Development. It increases the risk level in schedule wise, for instances if some key developers get sick in critical development phase. Unlike other agile methods, iteration is not tightly defined in Feature Driven Development. Eventually, some more tasks to be done in start-up phase for the process definition. (Rico et al. 2009, 69 – 73.)

Feature Driven Development is scalable for various types of projects; it defines practices and process for big teams also, and shows how to work multiple teams in parallel. But the iteration content is not as well defined as other agile methods do. In Feature Driven Development, testing is the mandatory part for the process and inspection is applied to remove defects and enhance the product quality. (Rico et al. 2009, 69 – 73.)

Customer feedback and iterative development component-by-component are addresses in Adaptive Software Development collaboration. There is a well-defined general guideline for development process in ASD. Through the general guidelines the project team can analyze and tailor the best suited practices which fit with the team requirements. On the other hand, the disadvantage is, the practices that are described in Adaptive Software Development are strict. So, the project team needs more work and time to apply the practices in the project. (Rico et al. 2009, 69 – 73.)

Among all agile methods, Dynamic System Development method is considered as a most formal agile method. In the development process, there is much architectural design in the beginning of the projects. Moreover, project team needs more documentation as well.

Testing is prioritized and each project team needs at least single test engineer that is a good sign for quality product. However, disadvantages of Dynamic System Development are, the described process seems very heavy, and the access of materials that are described in the practices are charged and controlled by Consortium. (Rico et al. 2009, 69 – 73.)

Chapter 4 – Scrum Methodologies

Scrum is an Agile framework for completing complex projects. Scrum originally was formalized for software development projects, but it works well for any complex, innovative scope of work. The possibilities are endless. The Scrum framework is deceptively simple.

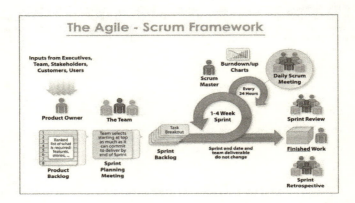

Figure 17: The Agile-Scrum Framework

Source: (Systems Plus Group, 2015)

Roles

Product Owner

The Scrum product owner is typically a project's key stakeholder. Part of the product owner responsibilities is to have a vision of what he or she wishes to build, and convey that vision to the scrum team. This is key to successfully starting any agile software development project. The agile product owner does this in part through the product backlog, which is a prioritized features list for the product. The product owner is commonly a lead user of the system or someone from marketing, product management or anyone with a solid understanding of users, the market place, the competition and of future trends for the domain or type of system being developed.

This, of course, varies tremendously based on whether the team is developing commercial software, software for internal use, hardware or some other type of product. The key is that the person in the product owner role needs to have a vision for what is to be built. Although the agile PO prioritizes the product backlog during the sprint planning meeting, the team selects the amount of work they believe they can do during each sprint, and how many sprints will be required.

The product owner does not get to say, "We have four sprints left, therefore you must do one-fourth of the product backlog this sprint." The Scrum product owner's job is to motivate the team with a clear, elevating goal. Team members know best what they are capable of, and so they select which user stories from the top of the product backlog they can commit to delivering during any sprint.In return for the Scrum team's commitment to completing the selected user stories from the top of the product backlog, the product owner makes a reciprocal commitment to not throw new requirements at the team during the sprint. Requirements can change (and change is encouraged) but only outside the sprint. Once the team starts on a sprint, it remains focused on the goal of that sprint.

The product owner role requires an individual with certain skills and traits, including availability, business savvy and communication skills.

First, the Scrum product owner needs to be available to his or her team. The best product owners show commitment by doing whatever is necessary to build the best product possible – and that means being actively engaged with their teams.

Business savvy is important for the agile product owner because he or she is the decision maker regarding what features the product will have. That means, the agile PO should understand the market, the customer and the business to make sound decisions.

Finally, communication is a large part of the product owner responsibilities. The product owner role requires working closely with key stakeholders throughout the organization and beyond, so he or she must be able to communicate different messages to different people about the project at any given time.

Scrum Master

A scrum master is the facilitator for an agile development team.

In product development, team members huddle together each morning for a stand-up meeting where they review progress and essentially restart the project. During the daily meetings, which are sometimes called "scrums," the scrum master asks the team members these three questions:

What did you do yesterday?

What will you do today?

Are there any impediments in your way?

Although the title of scrum master sounds powerful, the scrum master is not the project leader and is not held accountable for outcomes. The team as a whole is responsible for outcomes. The scrum master is responsible for:

Helping the team to reach consensus for what can be achieved during a specific period.

Helping the team to reach consensus during the daily scrum.

Helping the team to stay focused and follow the agreed-upon rules for daily scrums.

Removing obstacles that are impeding the team's progress.

Protecting the team from outside distractions.

Scrum Team

Responsible for the project's creation and delivery. The team members will normally be comprised of developers, QA, marketers, designers and wherever is needed to deliver a quality project. They are responsible for planning, design, development, testing, and project delivery.

Stakeholders

Represents a broad category of people who can be users, managers of users, operations, support,

Portfolio Managers, other Agile teams with dependencies, executive team, investors, and more.

Artifacts

Product Backlog

In the simplest definition, the Scrum Product Backlog is simply a list of all things that needs to be done within the project. It replaces the traditional requirements specification artifacts.These items can have a technical nature or can be user-centric(for instance: in the form of user stories).The owner of the Scrum Product Backlog is the Scrum Product Owner. The Scrum Master, the Scrum Team and other Stakeholders contribute it to have a broad and complete To-Do list.

Working with a Scrum Product Backlog does not mean that the Scrum Team is not allowed to create and use other artifacts. Examples for additional artifacts could be a summary of the various user roles, workflow descriptions, user interface guidelines, storyboards, or user interface prototypes. However, these artifacts do not replace the Scrum Product Backlog but complement and detail its content.

The Scrum Product Owner uses the Scrum Product Backlog during the Sprint Planning Meeting to describe the top entries to the team. The Scrum Team then determines which items they can complete during the coming sprint.

Each Scrum Product Backlog has certain properties that differentiate it from a simple to-do list:

1. An entry in the Scrum Product Backlog always add value for the customer

2. The entries in the Scrum Product Backlog are prioritized and ordered accordingly

3. The level of detail depends on the position of the entry within the Scrum Product Backlog

4. All entries are estimated

5. The Scrum Product Backlog is a living document

6. There are no action-items or low-level tasks in the Scrum Product Backlog

Only entries that add value

Each entry in the Scrum Product Backlog must have customer value. Entries without any customer value are pure waste and should not be present anyway. The Scrum Product Backlog can include entries for the exploration of customer needs or various technical options, a description of both functional and non-functional requirements, the work necessary to launch the product, and other items as well, such as setting up the environment or remediating defects. Some tasks may not add direct value to the functionality. Nevertheless, they might add value by increasing quality or reducing incidents in the long term.

Living document

The Scrum Product Backlog is changed throughout the whole project. If needed, new requirements are added and existing requirements may be modified, defined in more detail or even deleted. Requirements are no longer frozen early on. Instead the final set of requirements within the Scrum Product Backlog is also developed iteratively, together with the resulting software. This is different to traditional requirements engineering but allows maximizing customer value and minimizes development effort.

Different level of details

The requirements in the Scrum Product Backlog have a different level of details. Only those requirements that shall be implemented during one of the next sprints are defined in greater detail. The simple reason for this is that it does not make sense to invest time and effort into the specification of these requirements, as most of these requirements will have changed anyway until implementation starts.
No low-level tasks

The Scrum Product Backlog shall not contain the detailed requirement information. Ideally the final requirements are defined together with the customer during the sprint. Breakdown and distribution of these requirements is the responsibility of the Scrum Team.

The Scrum Product Backlog is ordered

All entries are prioritized and the Scrum Product Backlog is ordered. The Scrum Product Owner with the help of the Scrum Team does the prioritization. Added Value, Costs and Risks are the most common factors for prioritization. With this prioritization, the Scrum Product Owner decides what should be done next.
All entries are estimated

All the entries within the Scrum Product Backlog must be estimated according to the agreed definition (e.g. story points). This estimation can then be used to prioritize entries in the Scrum Product Backlog and to plan releases

Working with the Backlog

The backlog needs regular attention and care - it needs to be managed carefully. At the start of the project the Scrum Team and its Scrum Product Owner start by writing down everything they can think of easily. This is almost always more than enough for a first sprint.

After this initial setup, the Scrum Product Backlog has to be maintained in an ongoing process that comprises the following steps:

As new items are discovered they are described and added to the list. Existing ones are changed or removed as appropriate.

Ordering the Scrum Product Backlog. The most important items are moved to the top.

Preparing the high-priority entries for the next Sprint Planning Meeting

(Re-)Estimating the entries in the Scrum Product Backlog.

The Scrum Product Owner is responsible for making sure that the Scrum Product Backlog is in good shape this is a collaborative process. When using the Scrum Framework about 10% of the Scrum Teams total time should be reserved for maintaining the Scrum Product Backlog (discussion, estimation etc.) (http://www.scrum-institute.org/).

Figure 18: Albelli backlog board

Sprint Backlog

The Sprint Backlog is an ordered list of Product Backlog Items, preferably User Stories, that the Team believes it can complete during the coming Sprint. These items are pulled from the top of the Product Backlog during the Sprint Planning Meeting.

Each story should have a Point value assigned to it based on the Estimated amount of relative effort it will take to complete the story. It is important that the Team estimates in points and not hours. The Team determines how best to work through the Sprint Backlog. However, when possible, they should work on the highest value items first.

Once the Team forecasts the number of stories they feel they can accomplish in the Sprint Backlog, there should be no additions or changes until the Sprint ends. However, if during the Sprint management or the Product Owner decide there is a feature of higher business value that needs to come into the Sprint, the Product Owner should use the interruption procedure.

If an interruption arises that so dramatically changes the priorities or scope of the Sprint and cannot be dealt with as an interruption, the Product Owner may abort the Sprint. In this case the Team stops, a new Sprint Planning meeting is held and a new Sprint is started. This can be extremely disruptive to the Team so the Product Owner should be very leery of stopping mid-Sprint (https://www.scruminc.com/sprint-backlog/).

Product increment

The increment (or potentially shippable increment, PSI) is the sum of all the product backlog items completed during a sprint, integrated with the work of all previous sprints. At the end of a sprint, the increment must be complete, according to the scrum team's definition of done (DoD), fully functioning, and in a usable condition regardless of whether the product owner decides to release it.

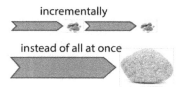

incrementally

instead of all at once

Figure 19: Product Increment

Source: (Sumiti, 2017)

Workflow

The Scrum process

A sprint (or iteration) is the basic unit of development in Scrum. The sprint is a timeboxed effort restricted to a specific duration. The duration is fixed in advance for each sprint and is normally between one week and one month, with two weeks being the most common.

Each sprint starts with a sprint planning event and ends with a sprint review and sprint retrospective

Scrum emphasizes working product at the end of the sprint that is really done. In the case of software, this likely includes that the software has been fully integrated, tested and documented, and is potentially shippable.

Sprint Planning

In Scrum, every iteration begins with a sprint planning meeting. At this meeting, the Product Owner and the team negotiate which stories a team will tackle that sprint. This meeting is a time-boxed conversation between the Product Owner and the team. It's up to the Product Owner to decide which stories are of the highest priority to the release and which will generate the highest business value, but the team has the power to push back and voice concerns or impediments.

When the team agrees to tackle the work, the Product Owner adds the corresponding stories into the sprint backlog.

At this point, the Product Owner may choose to leave while the team decomposes the forecasted backlog items into tasks. This meeting is sometimes called Sprint Planning Part 2. In Large Scale Scrum, multiple teams pull items from one Product Backlog. Multiple backlogs for one product, and multiple Product Owners lead to localize sub optimizations, longer work-in-progress queues, thus are harmful to agility.

The Daily Scrum

Every day, the Scrum team gathers in front of their task board to discuss the progress made yesterday, goals for today, and any impediments blocking their path.

What have I done since the last Scrum meeting (yesterday)?

What will I do before the next Scrum meeting (tomorrow)?

What prevents me from performing my work as well as possible?

This meeting should not exceed 15 minutes. If members of the team need to discuss an issue that cannot be covered in that amount of time, we recommend they attend a sidebar meeting following the stand-up. This allows team members to attend meetings that directly involve their work, instead of sitting through irrelevant meetings. Unfortunately, daily Scrums often last longer than 15 minutes. To compensate, many teams use stop watches or timers to uphold the time limitations. Also, to limit distracting small talk, many teams employ a talking stick or mascot, which a team member must hold to speak in the meeting. Upon finishing an update, the talking stick is then passed to the next team member, who reports, and so on.

Sprint Review

When the sprint ends, it's time for the team(s) to demonstrate a potentially shippable product increment to the Product Owner and other stakeholders. The Product Owner declares which items are truly done or not. Teams commonly discover that a story's final touches often excise the most effort and time. Partially done work should not be called"done."

This public demonstration replaces status meetings and reports, as those things do not aid transparency. Scrum emphasizes empirical observations such as working products.

Sprint Retrospective

After the sprint review meeting, the team and the Scrum Master get together in private for the retrospective meeting. During this meeting, the team inspects and adapts their process. When the Scrum Master and outer organization create an environment of psychological safety, team members can speak frankly about what occurred during the Sprint and how they felt about it. After all team members thoroughly understand each other, they work to identify what they'd like to do differently the next Sprint, typically focusing only on one or two specific areas of improvement each Sprint. The Scrum Master may also observe common impediments that impact the team and then work to resolve them (Schwaber & Sutherland, 2017).

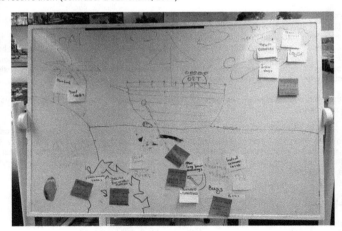

Figure 20: Albelli retrospective

Work & Delivery Flow-Example

We work with :   master branch

acceptance branch

testing branch

One branch per case

New case flow :

Figure 21: Case flow

Step 1: Drag it to WIP & Create new branch from Latest Master Branch: Naming the branch

PATCH: Fix bugs

REVISION: Improving existing features RELEASE: Adding new features MASTER RELEASE: Breaking changes

Number of sprint – PATCH/REV/ RELEASE - Case number Example: S018-REV-CMS-5903

TIP: After creating a branch remember to publish it and at the end of the day to push all your commits from your local HEAD branch to the chosen remote branch, so , in any case ,always someone from the team can pick it up and continue working with it.

Step 2: Coding / Merge Latest Master branch to yours if needed

Step 3: Code Review: Check your code changes with another member of the team

Step 4: Functional Review – Check your changes with the person who issued the problem

(example: Product owner, content team, merchandising, UX design, developer)

Merge it to the latest branch of acceptance. By pushing the latest branch, you automatically trigger the building process of your code in Team City. Check if passes all the unit tests and afterwards deploy to acceptance using AWS opsworks.
1. Set up a meeting so you can present & explain what you have done

2. Otherwise if it's a small change & easy to test it, ask them to check it and wait for them feedback

Step 5: Testing- Always make sure that you have clear explanation on how to set up section, so whoever picks this up has the all the information needed to test the case effectively. Step 6: Done –Always when merging with latest master branch update also the files CHANGELOG.md & ap-wp-config.php , so we can track all the code changes.

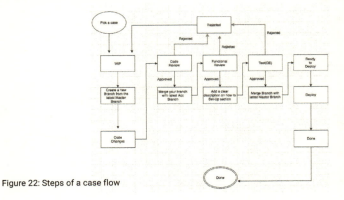

Figure 22: Steps of a case flow

Chapter 5 - Scrum Implementation

Scrum is a popular framework where complex products are being developed and sustained. It is a lightweight framework and easy to understand. The definition of Scrum can be addressed in this way, —A framework within which people can address complex adaptive problems, while productively and creatively delivering products of the highest possible value‖. (Schwaber, Kubacki, and Sutherland 2012, 136.)

Within Scrum's framework it is possible to employ various techniques and process. This process framework has been used to handle sophisticated product development since the early 1990s. Scrum ensures the relative efficiency of product management and development practices of developers so that the developers can improve. The Scrum framework is consisted with Scrum Team and their associated roles, rules, events, and artefacts. Within the Scrum framework each component serves a particular purpose and they are very important to Scrum's usage and success. (Schwaber et al. 2012, 136.)

The Scrum Theory

Empirical/experimental process control theory is the base of Scrum. Empiricism refers that the experience generates knowledge and making decisions based on what is known. Scrum assigns an incremental, iterative approach to control risk and optimize predictability. Transparency, inspection, and adaptation are the three pillars which uphold each implementation of empirical process control. Important aspects of the process should be visible to those responsible for the outcome. Transparency needs those aspects be addressed through a common standard so observers share a common knowledge of understanding of what is being observed. Scrum artifacts and progress toward a goal must be inspected by Scrum users to find out undesirable variances. The inspection should not be so frequent; inspections are most fruitful when diligently executed by proficient inspectors at the point of work. (Schwaber et al. 2012, 137.)

When any deviation of one or more aspects of a process is determined by the inspector and if the resulting product is not acceptable then the process or the processed material must be adjusted. A quick adjustment must be done to reduce further deviation. There are four formal opportunities prescribed by Scrum for inspection and adaption: Daily Scrum, Sprint Planning Meeting, Sprint Retrospective, and Sprint Review. (Schwaber et al. 2012, 138.)

The Scrum Team

The Scrum team consists of the Development Team, a Scrum Master, and a Product Owner. The teams are known as self-organizing and cross-functional. The team members of a self-organizing team select their best working strategies and they are not directed by someone else from outside. (Schwaber et al. 2012, 138)

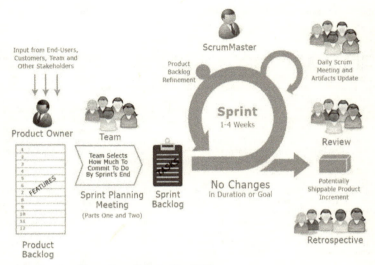

Graph 24: Function of Scrum Team (Agile Buddha 2015.)

Cross-functional teams offers all competencies needed to execute the task without relying on others not part of the team. Scrum's team model is designed to optimize creativity, productivity, and flexibility. Products are delivered iteratively and incrementally by the Scrum teams. (Schwaber et al. 2012, 138.)

The Product Owner

The Product Owner is responsible to maximize the value of the work of the Development Team and the product. It is only the Product Owner who is responsible for managing the Product Backlog. Management of Product Backlog includes: product backlog items are clearly expressed; ordering the item in the Product Backlog to best achieve goals and missions; ensuring the work performance value of the Development Team; making sure that the Product Backlog is transparent, visible, and clear to all, and determining the next task that Scrum Team will perform; and making sure that the Development Team is aware about the items in the Product Backlog to the level needed. (Schwaber et al. 2012, 138.)

Either the Product Owner or the Development Team may do the above mentioned works, but the Product Owner is still the accountable for these tasks. The entire organization must show respect on the decisions of the Product Owner, so the Product Owner can be succeeded. There is reflection of the Product Owner's desires/decisions in the content and Product Backlog ordering. It is not allowed that someone else would force the
Development Team to perform from a different set of requirements. (Schwaber et al. 2012, 139.)

The Development Team

A Development Team is consisted with a group of professionals who perform the tasks of delivering a potentially releasable Increment of ready product after each Sprint. The Increment is created by only Development Team members. It is structured and empowered a Development Team by the organization to organization and handles own work. A Development Team's overall effectiveness and efficiency are optimized by the resulting synergy. Development Teams are self-organizing. No one is allowed to tell them how to turn the Product Backlog's functionalities. The development team is cross-functional. There are no titles for Development Team members except developers, regardless of the task being executed by the person. Though the individual team members may be special for particular skills and areas, but it is the whole Development Team who is accountable for the deeds.There are no sub-teams under the Development Teams. (Schwaber et al. 2012, 139 – 140.)

The Scrum Master

It is Scrum Master who is responsible to ensure that Scrum is understood and enacted. However, to do these jobs Scrum Masters must ensure that the Scrum Team follows to Scrum theory, rules, and practices. The Scrum Master helps the Scrum Team to understand which interactions are helpful for the Scrum Team and which are not. The Scrum Master assists everyone to maximize the value which is created by the Scrum Team. (Schwaber et al. 2012, 140.)

The Product Owner is served by the Scrum Master in various ways, like: the Scrum Master helps the Product Owner by finding effective management techniques for Product Backlog. Scrum Master teaches the Scrum Team to make clear and concise Product Backlog items for the Product Owner. Clearly communicating goals, visions, and Product Backlog item to the Development Team. Long-term product planning is understood by the Scrum Master in an empirical environment. The Scrum Master helps in practicing and understanding agility. Scrum Master facilitates Scrum events as needed or requested. (Schwaber et al. 2012, 140 – 141.)

The Development Team is served by the Scrum Master in various ways, like: the Scrum Master helps the Development Team to be self-organizing and cross-functional. The Scrum Master leads and teaches the Development Team to develop high-value products. The Scrum Master helps to ensure the Development Team's progress by eliminating impediments. The Scrum Master facilitates Scrum events as needed or requested. The Development Team is coached in organizational environments in where the Scrum is not yet completely understood and adopted. (Schwaber et al. 2012, 141.)

The organization is served by the Scrum Master in various ways, like: the Scrum Master leads and coaches the organization for Scrum adoption. He/she Makes plan for Scrum implementation. The Scrum Master assists stakeholders and employees to understand and enact Scrum. Causing change that enhances the effectiveness of the Scrum Team. The Scrum Master works with other Scrum Masters to enhance the efficiency of the Scrum application in the organization. (Schwaber et al. 2012, 141.)

Scrum Events
In Scrum the referred events are used to create regularity and to reduce the need of unnecessary meetings which are not mentioned in Scrum. There are time-boxed events in Scrum so that each event gets a maximum duration. This makes sure an appropriate amount of time for each event and there is no waste of time in the planning process. In Scrum, the Sprint is like a container for all other events and each event is a formal opportunity to supervise and adapt something. (Schwaber et al. 2012, 141 – 142.)

The Sprint

The Sprint is like the heart of Scrum, it is a time-box of one month or less where a ready, useable, and releasable product increment is developed. A brand new sprint starts forthwith after the ending of the previous Sprint. The key parts of Sprints are: Daily Scrums, Sprint Planning Meeting, the Sprint review, the development work, and the Sprint Retrospective. During the Sprint, the changes which may affect the Sprint goal are not made; the composition of Development Team stays constant; and no decrementing of quality goals. (Schwaber et al. 2012, 142.)

Each Sprint is considered as a small project with maximum time duration of one month. Sprints are used to execute something just like projects. Each Sprint contains a definition about what is to be developed, a design and proper plan that would guide developing it, and the resultant product. Time duration of Sprint is limited with one calendar month. The definition of what is to be built may changes in case of long Sprint duration. Moreover, there is chance to increase the risk and complexity. (Schwaber et al. 2012, 142.)

It's possible to cancel a Sprint before the Sprint time-box is over, and it's only the Product Owner who is authorized to cancel the Sprint. When the Sprint goal becomes obsolete then the Sprint would be cancelled. This might happen if the company alters policy/direction or if technology or market conditions alter. The completed and ready Product Backlog items are reviewed after cancelling a Sprint. When the portion of the task is potentially releasable, typically the product is accepted by the Product Owner. The Product Backlog items are re-arranged and set back on the Product Backlog which is incomplete. It needs to regroup and manage another planning meeting for starting a new Sprint after cancellation a Sprint; as a result it consumes resources cancellation a Sprint. Actually Sprint cancellation is very uncommon and traumatic to the Scrum Team. (Schwaber et al. 2012, 142 – 143.)

The Sprint Planning Meeting

All the tasks what would be performed in the Sprint are planned first during the Sprint Planning Meeting. The sprint planning meeting is conducted by the Scrum Master, the Product Owner, and the entire Scrum Team. The stakeholders from outside may attend in the meeting, but it is very rare case in most companies. (Schwaber et al. 2012, 143.)

The Product Owner point out and describes the prioritized features to the Scrum Team during the planning meeting. The team and the Product Owner negotiate about the stories that would be tackled by the team in that Sprint. The conversation between the team and the Product Owner is a time-boxed conversation. It is the Product Owner who is the responsible to determine the highest prioritized stories to the release, but the team is authorized to push back and reveal their own opinions. The corresponding user stories are added into the sprint backlog by the Product Owner once the team agrees to handle the work. (Schwaber et al. 2012, 143.)

Daily Scrum

The development team arranges a 15-minute time-boxed event in every day to synchronize tasks and make a working plan for the next 24 hours. Every day at the same time and place the Daily Scrum is held. It is a very effective way to reduce complexity. Each team member answers the following questions during the meeting: What has been done since the last meeting? What would be accomplished before the next Scrum meeting? And what impedes me from executing my task as well as possible? (Schwaber et al. 2012, 145.)

The Daily Scrum is used to analyze progress towards the sprint goal and to analyze how progress is trending toward executing the task in the Sprint Backlog. After the Daily
Scrum, the Development Team meets to make a plan for rest of the Sprint's task. The Development Team should be able to explain the daily progress to the Scrum Master and Product Owner. (Schwaber et al. 2012, 145.)

The Daily Scrum is conducted by the Development Team but it is the Scrum Master who ensures that there is the meeting for the Development Team. The Development Team gets lessons from the Scrum Master about how to maintain the Daily Scrum within the 15minute time-box. The Daily Scrum is a significant event in Scrum development; it improves communications, reduces unnecessary meetings, inspects and removes obstacles to development, ensures quick decision making, and improves the knowledge level of the Development Team. (Schwaber et al. 2012, 146)

Sprint Review

The objective of Sprint Review is to inspect the increment and adjust the Product Backlog if needed. A Sprint Review is occurred at the end of the Sprint. During the Sprint Review, the stakeholders and the Scrum Team collaborate about what was accomplished in the Sprint. (Schwaber et al. 2012, 146.)

The included elements of Sprint Review are: what has been accomplished and what has not been accomplished are identified by the Product Owner. The Development Team identifies what went fine during the Sprint, what impediments it ran into, and the ways those impediments were eliminated. The executed work is demonstrated by the Development Team and they explain the answers of the questions about the Increment. The Product Owner negotiates about the existing Product Backlog. The entire group contributes to determine the next step, so that the subsequent Sprint Planning

Meetings get valuable input form the Sprint Review. The Sprint Review's result is known as the revised Product Backlog which demonstrates the Product Backlog items for the subsequent Sprint. (Schwaber et al. 2012, 146.)

Sprint Retrospective

For the Scrum Team, the Sprint Retrospective is a chance to inspect itself and make a plan for improvements to be enacted during the subsequent Sprint. And it occurs after the Sprint Review and before to the subsequent Sprint Planning Meeting. The Sprint Retrospective is a time-boxed meeting with three hours for one-month Sprints. However, proportionally less time is assigned for shorter Sprints. (Schwaber et al. 2012, 147.)

The objectives of the Sprint Retrospective are: detect how the last Sprint went with regards to relationships, people, process, and tools; identifying and ordering the major items which went well and potentially improved; and developing an effective plan for the Scrum Team so that the Scrum Team can operates its works flexibly. (Schwaber et al. 2012, 147.)

The Scrum Master motivates the Scrum team so that the Scrum Team can improve within the Scrum process framework, and create its work enjoyable and effective for the subsequent Sprint. The Scrum Team creates plan about how to develop the product quality during each Sprint Retrospective. Actually the improvements that would be implemented in the next Sprint should be identified by the Scrum Team by the end of the Sprint Retrospective. (Schwaber et al. 2012, 147.)

Scrum Artifacts

Scrum artifacts define work or value in different ways which are effective in providing opportunities and transparency for inspection and adaptation. Scrum's defined Artifacts are designed specially to increase transparency of important information needed to make sure that the Scrum Teams are successful to deliver an accomplished Increment. (Schwaber et al. 2012, 147.)

Product Backlog

Product Backlog is a list of prioritized features and this list contains information of all functionality needed in the product. The Product Owner is the sole person who is responsible for the Product Backlog. It is dynamic and never complete. The Product Backlog constantly changes to detect what the product needs to be competitive, appropriate, and useful. The Product Backlog exists, as long as a listed product exists. (Schwaber et al. 2012, 148.)

The Product Backlog contains all functions, features, enhancement, requirements, and creates the plan that would be applied to the product for any changes in future releases. The items of Product Backlog contain the attributes of an order, description, and estimate.
The Product Backlog is ordered by priority, risk, value, and necessity. The Product Backlog items which are top-ordered are taken into account to develop first. (Schwaber et al. 2012, 148.)

Among the Product Backlog items, the top-ordered items are more detailed and clearer than lower-ordered ones. The Product Backlog items that would be taken into action in the upcoming Sprint by the Development Team are fine-grained, having been decomposed so that any one item can be accomplished within the Sprint time-boxed. Changes in the technology, market conditions, or business requirements may cause changes in the Product Backlog. (Schwaber et al. 2012, 148 – 149.)
The Product Backlog grooming is an on-going process in which the Development Team and Product Owner collaborate on the details of Product Backlog items. It is the act of adding information, estimates, and order to items in the Product Backlog. The items are reviewed and revised during the Product Backlog grooming. But it is possible to update the items at any time and only the Product Owner can perform this. The Scrum team decides how and when the grooming would be executed. During the Sprint, the grooming is a parttime activity between the Development Team and the Product Owner. (Schwaber et al. 2012, 149.)

Sprint Backlog

The Sprint Backlog is known as the set of Product Backlog items that are chosen for the Sprint along with a plan of delivery of the product increment and realizing the Sprint goal. It is a forecast about the type of functionality that would be taken into account in the subsequent Increment and the tasks needed to deliver that functionality; and this forecast is made by the Development Team. The Sprint Backlog refers the set of works what would be performed by the Development Team to turn Product Backlog Items into an accomplished Increment. Moreover, the Sprint Backlog makes the work visible which is identified by the Development Team and this work is needed to achieve the Sprint goal. (Schwaber et al. 2012, 149 – 150.)

Throughout the Sprint the Sprint Backlog is been modified by the Development Team, and it emerges during the Sprint. The Development Team adds the work to the Sprint Backlog whenever it needs to add new work. As work is accomplished or performed, the estimated rest of the work is updated. The plan's elements are removed whenever it deems unnecessary. During a Sprint, only the Development Team can alter its Sprint Backlog. It is highly visible a Sprint Backlog, and it is the real-time picture of the task that the Development Team intends to execute during the Sprint, and it belongs only to the Development Team. (Schwaber et al. 2012, 149 – 150.)

Increment

The concept of increment is very important in agile software development. In Scrum, the maintenance of increment is the key of a project success. The sum of the completed Product Backlog items during a Sprint and all previous Sprints is known as the Increment.

Whenever a Sprint ends a new Increment must be done. (Schwaber et al. 2012, 150.)

Chapter 6 - Conclusion

This book explains all important aspects of agile, and provides theory about what agile is and what is contains. There is bunch of information of all important agile methods and practices which helps to evaluate and select the best agile methods and practices for a development team. The survey part demonstrates all practical information of agile practices in current world. Moreover, the survey shows that the traditional methods are no longer effective and agile methods are getting popular day by day. Scrum is the most popular method among the developers and organizations. This book provides a complete guideline about Scrum which is effective for selecting the Scrum as the software development method.

There are different types of agile methods and practices for software development. They are not equal in strength, flexibility, weakness, risk, and usage. Scrum is a lightweight development method with long sprints and its popularity is growing day by day. Extreme Programming provides a robust methodology for release planning, and it is considered to be low risk. Many developers like to combine practices from Scrum and Extreme Programming and apply them in software development.

Feature Driven Development method has some flexibility and this method is based on a traditional object-oriented design method with good quality controls. Crystal Methods offers a good blend of agile practices with only moderate risk. It has a large number of traditional and agile practices. It had been designed to be scalable. Dynamic System Development is still very popular in United Kingdom. This method is product focused with wide range of practices. The practices are with low risk but not flexible. Adaptive Software Development is especially for complex and large software development project. In this development method, the project is carried out in cycle.

Software engineering is a disciplined, systematic, and quantifiable approach for developing software. Similarly, agile methods are disciplined, systematic, and quantifiable approach for building software products. Agile methods adapt the values of customer collaboration, adaptability, and iterative development to change to the development of software products to satisfy customers.

A very important thing we can learn from this book that agile methods should not be judged on the basis of their size or how much they resemble to traditional methods. Rather agile methods should be judged on the basis of strength of their individual practices. For example, the release planning methodology of Extreme Programming is the best among all agile methods and this method contains some key practices as well. Large sized agile methods may enhance risk as it is challenging to adopt a large number of practices in software development process. Moreover, large never guarantees low risk. Therefore, justin-time, just-enough, and right-sized agile practices with adaptable and flexible process may be effective for a development team.

Bibliography & References

English bibliography

Abrahamsson, P. (2003). New directions on agile methods: a comparative analysis. Adzic, G. (2009). Bridging the Communication Gap: Specification by Example and Agile Acceptance Testing. Neuri Limited.

Adzic, G. (2011). How successful teams deliver the right software. Manning. Specification by example: ISBN 978-0-321-27865-4.

Agile Alliance. (2001). Manifesto for Agile Software Development. webpage: Manifesto-for-Agile-Software-Dev.

Alternaltive definition of Business Analysis from BCS ISEB. . (2008).

Beck, K. (2002). Test Driven Development: By Example. Addison-Wesley Professional.

Beck, K. (2003). Test-Driven Development by Example. Addison Wesley - Vaseem.

Behaviour-Driven Development. (2012). Retrieved 12 August 2012. .

Bellware, S. (2008). "Behavior-Driven Development". Code Magazine. . Retrieved 12

August 2012.

Booch, G. (1991). Object Oriented Design: With Applications. . Benjamin Cummings. : p. 209. ISBN 9780805300918. Retrieved 2014-08-18. .

Chelimsky, D., Dave, A., Zach, D., A Aslak, H., Bryan, H., & North, D. (2001). The RSpec Book:

Behaviour Driven Development with RSpec, Cucumber, and Friends. . The Pragmatic Bookshelf.

Cockburn, A. (s.d.). Crystal Clear, A Human-Powered Methodology for Small Teams .

Cohn, M. (2005). "Agile Estimating and Planning". Mountain Goat Software. Retrieved 2008-02-01.

Cohn, M. (2016). Planning Poker Cards: Effective Agile Planning and Estimation . Mountain

Goat Software.: Retrieved 30 March 2016.

Design Patterns and Refactoring. (s.d.).

Diethelm, I., Geiger, L., & Zündorf, A. (2004). "Systematic story driven modeling: a case study". Third International Workshop on Scenarios and State Machines: 65–70.

Eickhoff, C., Geiger, N., Hahn, M., & Zündorf, A. (2012). "Developing Enterprise Web Applications Using the Story Driven Modeling Approach". . Current Trends in Web Engineering. LNCS (7059): 196–210.

Feathers, M. (2004). Working Effectively with Legacy Code . Prentice Hall.

Haring, R., & de Ruiter, R. (2011). Behavior Driven development: Beter dan Test Driven Development. Java Magazine (in Dutch): . Veen Magazines (1): 14–17. ISSN 1571-6236.

Henry, J., & Henry, S. (1993). Quantitative assessment of the software maintenance process and requirements volatility. In Proc. of the ACM Conference on Computer Science,. pages 346–351.

Highsmith, J. (2000). Adaptive Software Development: A Collaborative Approach to Managing Complex Systems. New York: Dorset House, 392pp, ISBN 0-932633-40-4 .

Highsmith, J., & Addison-Wesley. (2004). Agile Project Management: Creating Innovative Products. March 2004,: 277pp, ISBN 0-321-21977-5

Hopp, W. J. (2004). "To Pull or Not to Pull: What Is the Question?". Manufacturing &

Service Operations Management: 133.

Kanban. (2011). Random House Dictionary. . Dictionary.com.: Retrieved April 12, 2011.

Kathleen, B. H., Vander, R. ,., & Kimi, Z. (2008). From Analyst to Leader: Elevating the Role of the Business Analyst Management Concepts". As the discipline of business analysis becomes professionalized": ISBN 1-56726-213-9. p94.

Kent, B. (2012). "Why does Kent Beck refer to the "rediscovery" of test-driven development?". Retrieved December 1,2014.

Kerievsky, J. (2004). Refactoring to Patterns. Addison Wesley.

Krajewski, L. J., & Ritzman, L. P. (2005). Operations Management: Processes and Value Chains. Pearson Education, Upper Saddle River.

Lee, C. (2001). "Extreme Programming". Computerworld. . Retrieved January 11, 2011. Luo, X., Slotegraaf, R. J., & Xing, P. (2006). "Cross-Functional "Coopetition":The Simultaneous Role of Cooperation and Competition Within Firms". Journal of Marketing.

American Marketing Association., 70: 67–80. ISSN 1547-7185.

Muckstadt, J., & Tayur, S. (1995). "A comparison of alternative kanban control mechanisms. II. Experimental results". IIE Transactions. 27 (2): 151–161. doi:10.1080/07408179508936727.

Newkirk, J., & Vorontsov, A. (2004). Test-Driven Development in Microsoft . NET, Microsoft Press.

Norbisrath, Z. J., & Ulrich, A. R. (2013). Story Driven Modeling. Amazon Createspace. . p. 333. ISBN 9781483949253.

Ohno. (1998). Toyota Production System - beyond large-scale production. Taiichi (June 1988): Productivity Press. p. 29. ISBN 0-915299-14-3.

Pugh, K. (2011). Lean-Agile Acceptance Test-Driven Development: Better Software Through Collaboration. . Addison-Wesley. ISBN 978-0321714084.

Ramsey, W. L., Bourque, D., & Dupuis, P. R. (2001). . Integrating pair programming into a software development process. 14th Conference on Software Engineering Education and Training. Charlotte. (February 19–20, 2001). pp. 27–36. doi:10.110.

Richards, K. (2007). Agile project management: running PRINCE2 projects with DSDM . Ryser, J., & Glinz, M. (2000). "Improving the Quality of Requirements with

Scenarios".Proceedings of the Second World Congress on Software Quality.

Yokohama: 55–60.

Schonberger, R. (2001). Let's Fix It! . New York: Overcoming the Crisis in Manufacturing. :

Free Press. pp. 70–71.

Shingō, S. (1989). A Study of the Toyota Production System from an Industrial Engineering Viewpoint. Productivity Press. . p. 228. ISBN 0-915299-17-8.

Solis, C., & Wang, X. (2011). "A Study of the Characteristics of Behaviour Driven

Development". Software Engineering and Advanced Applications (SEAA). 37th EUROMICRO Conference on: 383–387. doi:10.1109/SEAA.2011.76.

Takeuchi, H., & Nonaka, I. (1986). New New Product Development Game. Harvard Business Review. : Retrieved June 9, 2010. Moving the Scrum Downfield .

Tayur, S. (1992). "Properties of serial kanban systems". . Queueing Systems.: 12 (3-4): 297–

318. doi:10.1007/BF01158805.

Tayur, S. (1993). "Structural Properties and a Heuristic for Kanban-Controlled Serial Lines".

Management Science. 39 (11): 1347–1368. doi:10.1287/mnsc.39.11.1347 .

Tharayil, R. (2016). "When to embrace, Behaviour Driven Development (BDD)?".

SolutionsIQ. Retrieved 15 February 2016.

Van Gorp, P. (2008). "Evaluation of the Story Driven Modeling Methodology: From Towers to Models". Technical Report University of Antwerp.

Verheyen, G. (2016). "Scrum: Framework, not methodology". . Gunther Verheyen. Gunter Verheyen.: Retrieved February 24,2016. .

Virine, L., & Trumper, M. (2007). Project Decisions: The Art and Science. Management

Concepts. . .ISBN 978-1-56726-217-9.

Waldner, J.-B. (1992). Principles of Computer-Integrated Manufacturing. London: John

Wiley. pp. 128–132. ISBN 0-471-93450-X. .

Yasuhiro Monden. (1998). Toyota Production System, An Integrated Approach to Just-In-Time. Third edition, Norcross, GA: Engineering & Management Press,: ISBN 0-412-83930-X. .

Zündorf, A., Schürr, A., & Winter, A. J. (1999).). "Story Driven Modeling". University of Paderborn: Technical Report (tr-ri-99-211).

Websites

1. http://agilemanifesto.org/principles.html.

2. http://martinfowler.com/articles/newMethodology.html .

"Business Analysis Body of Knowledge v2.0". (2008). IBA. : Retrieved 2012-08-26. . "Planning poker - Trademark, . (2008). Trademark Status & Document Retrieval

(TSDR).Service Mark #3473287".: Retrieved 2014-05-26.

"Story Test-Driven Development". (2013). Retrieved 2013-04-15. "Velocity:Measuring and Planning an Agile Project". (2010). Retrieved 2010-09-24. (2017, 5 12). Récupéré sur http://dddcommunity.org :
3. http://dddcommunity.org
Example Driven Design". . (2013). Retrieved 2013-04-15.

Extreme Programming" USFCA-edu-601-lecture. (n.d.).
4. http://leadinganswers.typepad.com/. (2017, 11 11). Project "You" and Project "Two".

5. http://leadinganswers.typepad.com/: http://leadinganswers.typepad.com/
6. http://www.agilenutshell.com. (2017, 12 8). Agile in a Nutshell, What is agile.
7. http://www.agilenutshell.com: http://www.agilenutshell.com

What is Scrum? An Agile Framework for Completing Complex Projects - Scrum Alliance. Scrum Alliance. (2016). Retrieved February 24, 2016.

www.wavemaker.com. (n.d.). What is Rapid Application Development model? Retrieved from: https://www.wavemaker.com/rapid-application-development-model/
8.http://leadinganswers.typepad.com/photos/uncategorized/2007/06/28/1_lifecycle_2.jpg(figure 2)

9. http://agilemanifesto.org/principles.html)(figure 3)
10. http://www.pmconsult.it/dynamic-system-development-method.html(figure 10)